PROVENCE
FOOD AND WINE
THE ART OF LIVING

FRANÇOIS MILLO AND **VIKTORIJA TODOROVSKA**

SURREY
BOOKS

AN AGATE IMPRINT

CHICAGO

Photo on p. 81 courtesy of Xavier Mathieu
Photo on p. 115 courtesy of Thierry Thiercelin
Photo on p. 121 courtesy of The Setai, Miami Beach
Photo on p. 147 courtesy of M. Bouko
Photo on p. 160 by Caterina Prochilo
All other photos by François Millo

Printed in China.

Provence Food and Wine: The Art of Living
First printing, March 2014
Trade paperback ISBN-13: 978-1-57284-158-1
Ebook ISBN-13: 978-1-57284-735-4

Library of Congress Cataloging-in-Publication Data is on file at the Library of Congress.

10 9 8 7 6 5 4 3 2 1

Surrey is an imprint of Agate Publishing. Agate books are available in bulk at discount prices.
For more information, go to agatepublishing.com.

Contents

Welcome to Provence

A LAND OF SUNSHINE, LUMINOUS LIGHT, AZURE SEA, and iconic lavender fields, Provence is where travelers go to dream, and dream to return. It is a land of strong traditions and a blend of cultures, a home to generous and passionate people who know how to celebrate life and who practice *l'art de vivre*, the timeless art of living that feeds the soul.

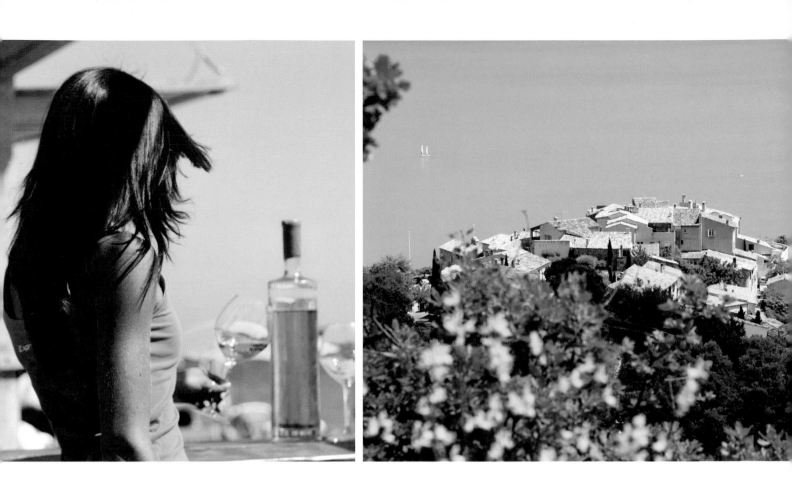

THIS SUN-DRENCHED LAND OF VARIED LANDSCAPES AND
vibrant colors reveals layers of beauty, from the desert-like plateaus of
Haute Provence to the beaches of Cannes, Saint-Tropez, and Nice. To
truly experience it, you need to see, touch, and taste Provence. Let us
open the door to this enchanting land, which will captivate you forever.

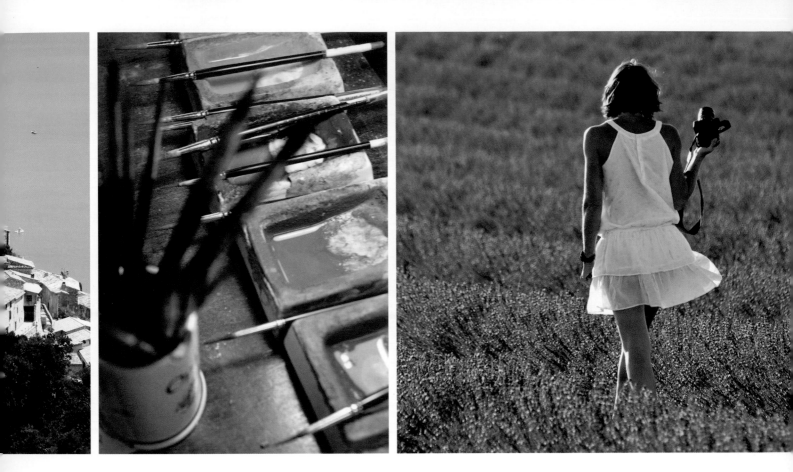

HISTORY AND GEOGRAPHY

When they think of Provence, most travelers imagine the Mediterranean, lavender fields, and stone houses with blue shutters—but there is so much more to Provence than these iconic images. This sunny part of southern France stretches from the Mediterranean to the hills of Haute Provence, and from the Rhône River valley to the Alps, with hundreds of small villages scattered in between and matchless beauty every step of the way.

Provence's climate and landscape are quite diverse: limestone mountains, deep canyons, high plateaus covered in lavender, mountaintop medieval villages, and beautiful coastline are all bathed in sun and caressed by sea breezes, but also swept clean by the strong *Mistral* (a cold wind that blows mostly in the winter and spring).

Rosé, the countryside, art, lavender—Provence reveals its secrets only to the most dedicated travelers.

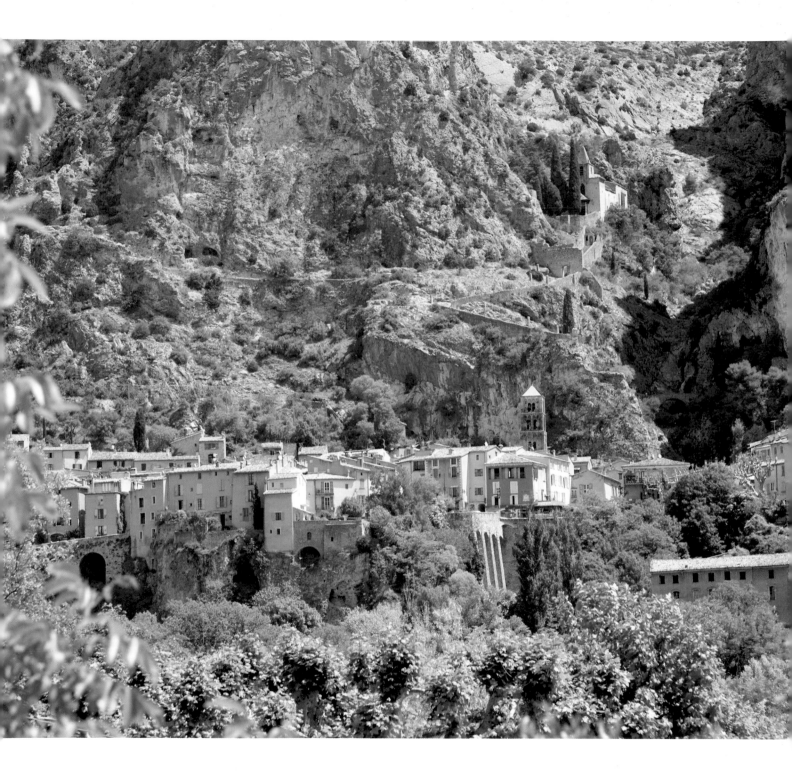

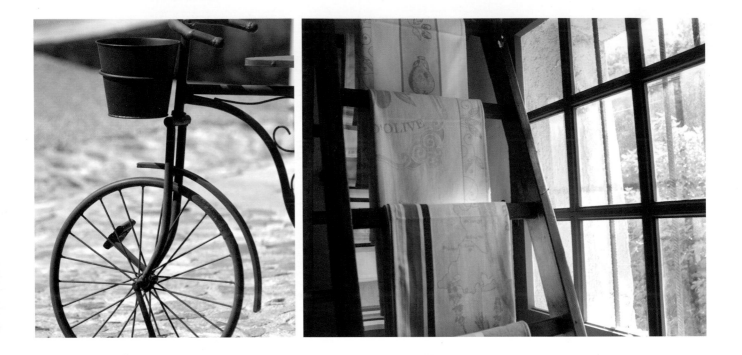

Provence has a long and illustrious history. In the sixth century BCE, the Phocaeans, Greek sailors from Asia Minor, landed on the coast of Provence and founded the city of Marseille (then known as Massalia), one of France's oldest cities. Thus began the history of this complex region and the production of some of its most iconic commodities: wine and olive oil.

Four centuries later, the Romans arrived and founded their first province outside Rome: La Provincia Romana, which is the origin of its present-day name, Provence. After the fall of the Roman Empire and the Vandal attacks that plagued Europe for centuries, Provence was a semi-independent state ruled by a succession of counts until the mid-fifteenth century. In 1486, it was legally incorporated into the kingdom of France.

Today, Provence is a modern region with large cities, winding roads, and thriving industry. Although it has now been a part of France for five centuries, Provence has nevertheless maintained a strong identity, unique traditions, varied languages, and healthy lifestyle. At its core, Provence's culture has been forged by diverse influences and the timeless art of living, which the Provençals practice with passion and dedication.

THIS PAGE: The little details reveal an area's heritage and art of living.

OPPOSITE PAGE: Nestled at the foot of the Alps, the village of Moustiers-Sainte-Marie overlooks the Gorges du Verdon.

LAVENDER

One of the oldest-known herbs, lavender is part of the soul of Provence. The vibrant purple that blankets the region's hills from June to August is the first thing most of us think of at the mention of Provence.

Lavender has grown wild in Provence for more than 2,000 years. The Romans knew its therapeutic properties well and used it to perfume relaxing, healing baths. In the Middle Ages, the Provençals used the herb to treat the sick and wounded. In the twentieth century, lavender began to be commercially cultivated for France's world-famous perfume industry. *Parfumeries* Fragonard and Molinard, both founded in the town of Grasse, still use Provençal lavender in their fragrances.

Provence's sunny climate and dry, rocky soils provide a perfect home for the plant. In 1981, lavender grown at high altitudes in Haute Provence was granted *Appellation d'Origine Contrôlée* (AOC; translates in English to "Controlled Designation of Origin") status. As with wine, an AOC defines the area where lavender can be grown and specifies how it is to be harvested and distilled.

At small, traditional Provençal farms where lavender has been grown for many generations, the herb is still harvested by hand with sickles. The flowers are then dried for days before they are distilled. The distillation process involves running steam through stills full of dried lavender, thus yielding precious essential oils. About 300 pounds of lavender are needed to make a single quart of essential oil.

Lavender perfume, one of the most potent natural fragrances, soothes the body and soul, eases tension, and enhances sleep. L'Occitane en Provence, the well-known skincare and beauty-product company founded in Provence, has successfully spread lavender's fame around the world.

Lavender also finds its way into Provençal cuisine, infusing ice cream, sorbets, and custards, and adding aroma and flavor to savory dishes. From vinaigrettes to roasted chicken, this symbol of Provence permeates everything Provençal, imprinting lasting memories on the senses.

The perfume industry is the main driver of lavender cultivation. When summer begins, the Provençal hills turn a spectacular shade of blue, a color that lends itself well to a little romance.

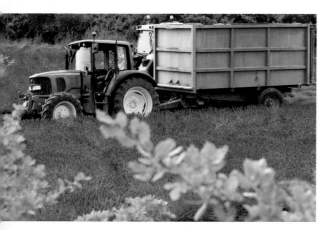

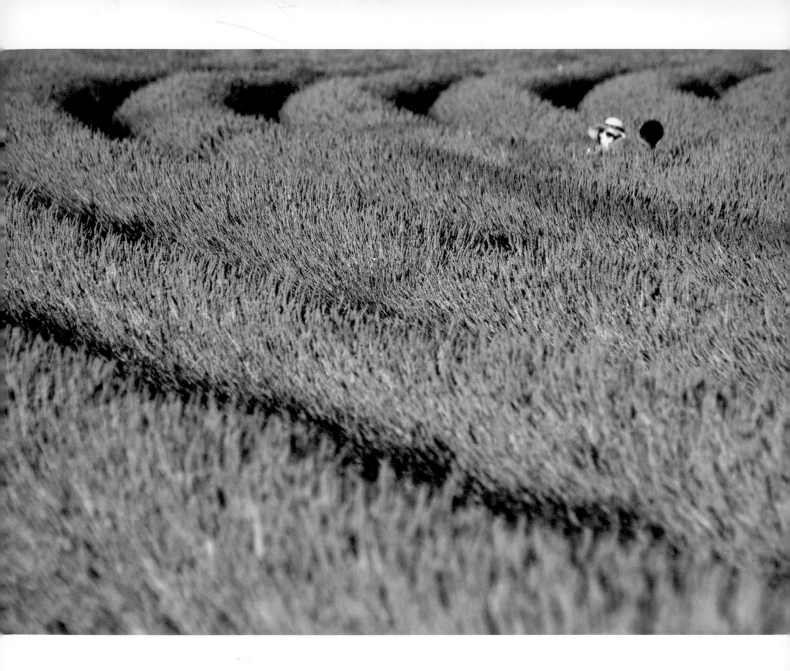

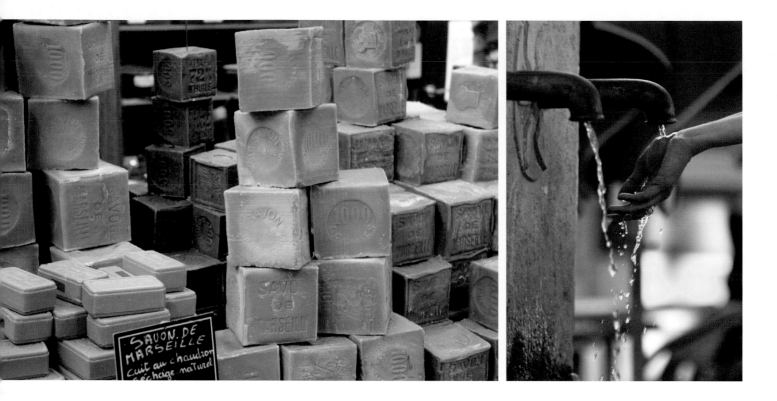

THIS PAGE: In the villages of Provence, laundry used to be washed in the public fountains with Marseille soap.

OPPOSITE PAGE: *Pétanque* is a very serious affair that requires great concentration.

MARSEILLE SOAP

World-famous *savon de Marseille* (Marseille soap) has a history that goes back more than 600 years. The first-known mention of making soap in the area is from a document written in the year 1370. The industry was so important that in 1688, Louis XIV passed a law specifying that only soap made from olive oil using traditional methods could be called Marseille soap. Engaging in fraud was punishable by expulsion from Provence—a harsh sentence, indeed!

Today, only a few *savonneries* (soap factories) make the legendary soap in the traditional manner. But as the world is discovering the moisturizing properties of *savon de Marseille* and its exquisite benefits for sensitive skin, this treasure of Marseille is regaining popularity. A true Provençal product, born of the bounty of the olive tree, the sun, and the sea, Marseille soap is as good for the planet as it is for the skin, as it is hypoallergenic and biodegradable.

Great care on the part of the *maître savonnier* (soap master) is necessary to make *savon de Marseille*. It starts as a blend of olive oil, Mediterranean

sea water, and soda ash heated in large cauldrons and constantly stirred for ten straight days. The liquid is then poured into open pits, cut into bars, and stamped before hardening completely. The sun and the *Mistral*, two elements Provence abounds in, help complete the drying process, which can take as long as a month.

PÉTANQUE

You can't think of Provence without thinking of *pétanque*. This symbol of the Provençal *art de vivre*, played by people of all ages in every town square, is part of every story and vacation memory about Provence.

The ancient Greeks played a similar game using rounded stones. They brought the game, along with the grapevine, to Marseille around 600 BCE. The original game, which involved longer distances and players taking a coordinated set of steps as they launched the ball, is still played today in Provence. Over the past century, the game gradually evolved into what we know today as *pétanque*, which is played at much shorter distances (20 to 30 feet), and is simple, convivial, and easy to play outdoors.

The name *pétanque* comes from the Provençal *pèd tanco*, which means "feet firmly planted on the ground." Legend has it that one summer evening in 1910, Jules Lenoir, a resident of Provence who was unable to play the strictly choreographed version of the game, which required forward or lateral movement along a long court, planted his feet on the ground and played anyway. *Pétanque* as it is known today, a simpler game requiring much less physical exertion, was born.

Pétanque is played on hard dirt or gravel clearings found in most Provençal towns. The goal of the game is to throw metal balls as close as possible to a small wooden ball called a *cochonnet* (literally, "piglet") while standing with both feet planted inside a circle. Important note for the uninitiated: *Pétanque* is played to 13 points, and if a team loses 13 to 0, they must "*embrasser Fanny*," which involves kissing the behind of a nude female statue (Fanny) that's generally located near the *pétanque* court. A poster of a buxom lady is used in the event there is no statue. The punishment is delivered immediately and in public!

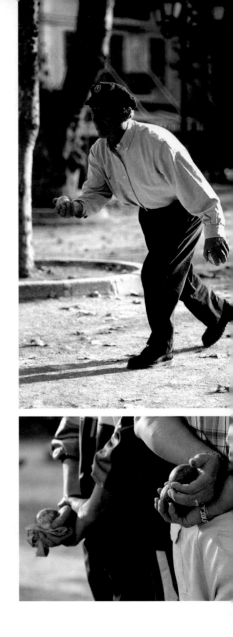

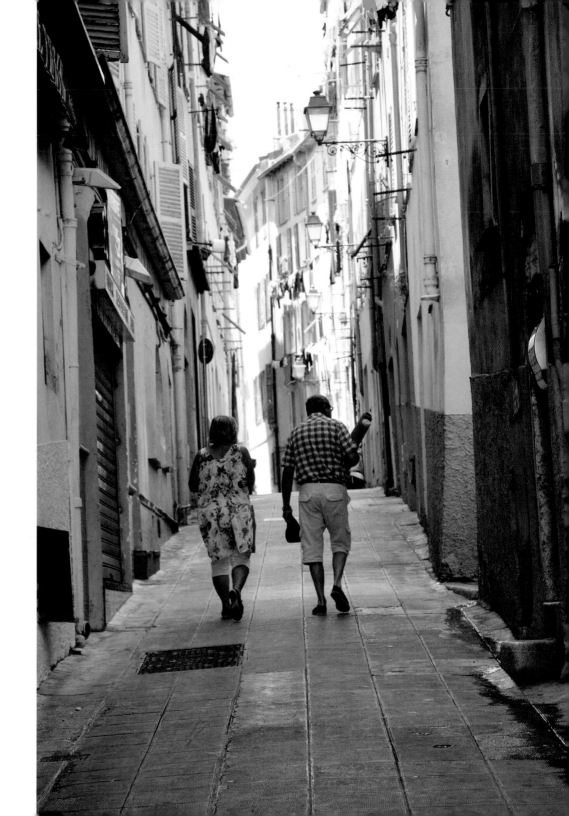

The best places to overhear the two regional dialects are in the small side streets and outdoor markets of Provence.

Today, playing *pétanque* is as much a part of Provence as the fountains you'll find in the middle of every village, rosé wine, and the local bars found throughout every town. There's one other important point we can't help but mention: *Pétanque* is the only sport you can play while holding a glass of rosé!

PROVENÇAL AND NIÇOIS

La langue provençale, a blend of Latin and sunshine, is the product of several old local dialects intermingled with Latin during the long Roman presence in Provence. It remains the traditional language of Provençals, lending zest and vivacity to market conversations, familial chats, and, of course, games of *pétanque*, as well as literature and other creative forms of expression.

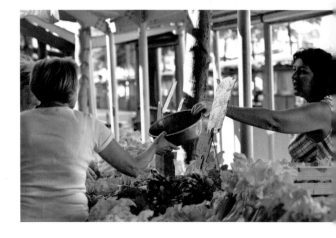

In the first millennium, when Latin was Provence's official written language, Provençal was the spoken language of the population. In the Middle Ages (eleventh to fifteenth centuries), the Troubadours wrote poetry in Provençal, strengthening its role. In the fifteenth century, when Provence became part of the kingdom of France, French was imposed as the written language; it continued to dominate through the seventeenth and eighteenth centuries. French became the language of literature and was enshrined in the first encyclopedias as the official written language of France, while Provençal was relegated to a lesser role.

In the nineteenth century, Nobel laureate Frédéric Mistral breathed new life into the language by simplifying the Provençal writing system, writing a Provençal dictionary, and, most importantly, translating great literature into Provençal. The *lengo prouvençalo*, spoken by many Provençals to this day, is thus founded on a rich literary tradition.

Recognized as a language belonging to the Oc family of languages spoken in the south of France, Provençal is related to Niçois, which is spoken in what was historically known as the earldom of Nice. Niçois (also known as Nizzardo, Nissart, and Niçard) has stronger influences from the dialects of Liguria, a region

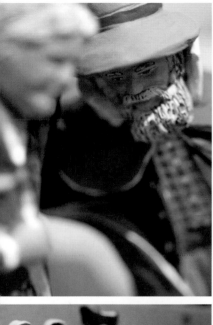

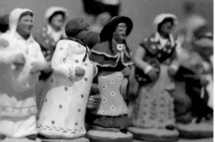

Santons reflect the simplicity of a bygone era.

of neighboring Italy. In 1996, both Provençal and Niçois were recognized by UNESCO as endangered languages.

Today, Provençal has its own grammar books, dictionaries, and literature. It is taught at universities in France and abroad and also continues to live on in musical expressions both traditional and modern. Of course, the best way to learn Provençal is still to join in a game of *pétanque*—preferably one fortified with pastis—and enjoy the *art de vivre*.

SANTONS

Santons, or *santouns* (little saints) in Provençal, are vibrant, hand-painted clay figurines featured in traditional Provençal nativity scenes. These popular souvenirs have become ambassadors of the region's traditions.

Santons emerged in the eighteenth century, after the French Revolution suppressed observance of midnight mass on Christmas Eve and families started creating their own nativity scenes at home. In typical Provençal fashion, the traditional nativity scene was enriched with figurines representing the characters of village life in Provence: the scissors grinder, the fishwife, the blind man, the bread maker, the chestnut seller, and so on. To this day, these brightly painted figurines, each with a story that can be read in his or her face and attire, adorn Provençal homes during the holidays, evoking memories of magic and tradition.

Today, the making of *santons* is a family craft handed down from parents to children. The company Santons Fouque, in Aix-en-Provence, has carried on a tradition of handcrafting the figurines for four generations. At the company's studio, which is also a museum and shop, visitors can learn about the craft of making *santons*. It starts with molding clay into figurines and then adding accessories, such as baskets and hats. The *santons* are then dried and fired in a kiln, after which they are hand-painted in vibrant Provençal colors. The rich colors breathe life into the figurines. At Christmastime, *santons* brighten up homes in Provence and around the world, bringing together tradition and fun.

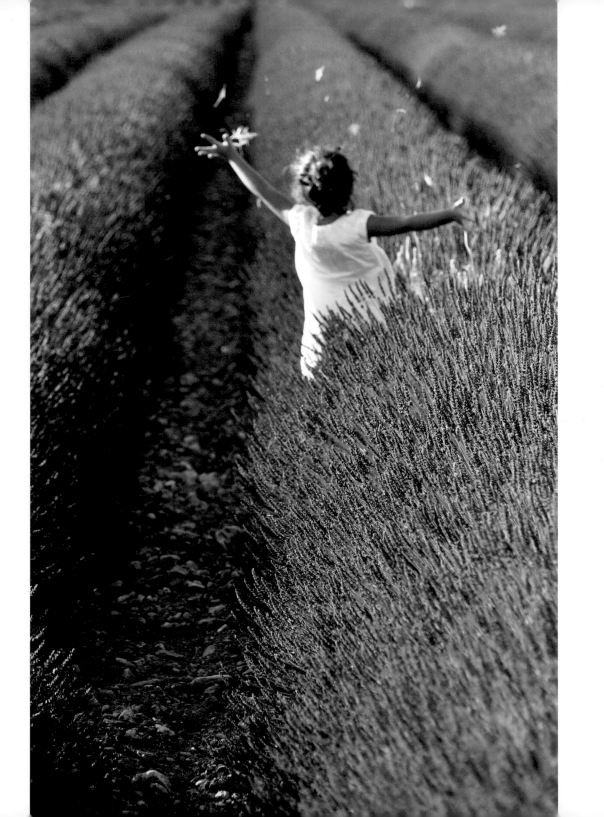

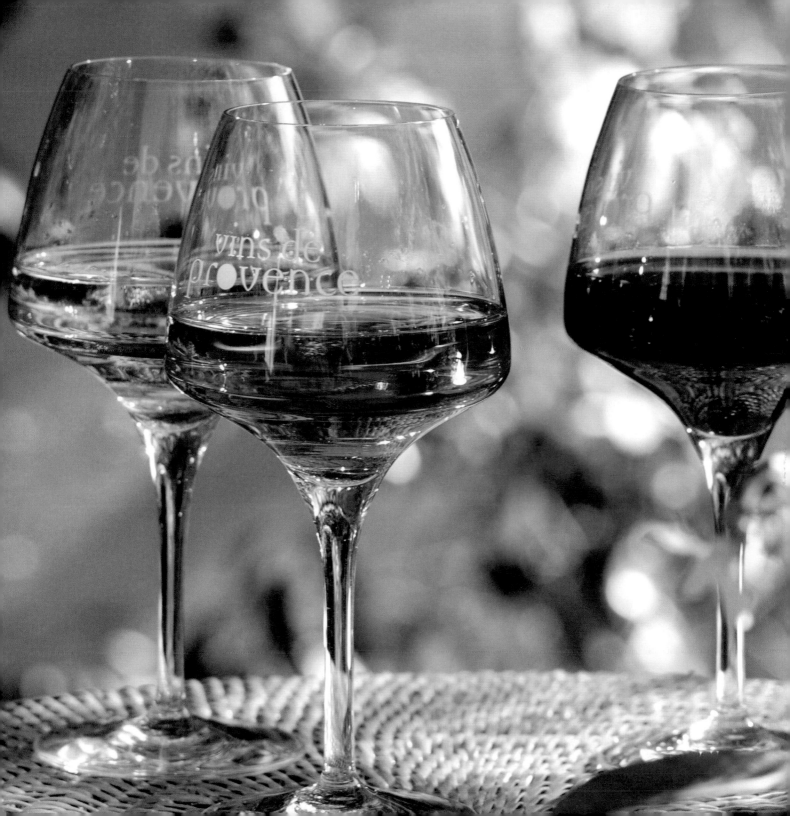

Provence Wine

PROVENCE IS A DIVERSE AND SURPRISING REGION. BEST KNOWN for its sea and sun, it is also a land of rocky hills, mountains, wilderness, near-desert landscapes, and a luminosity that captures the spirit. It holds many secrets, and slowly reveals them only to those who are patient enough to seek them out. The same holds true of its wines: rosés with a distinct personality; elegant whites; and smooth, memorable reds hail from this sunny region on the edge of the Mediterranean. Most of the wine produced in Provence today is rosé, a lovely pale pink wine famous for being lively, dry, aromatic, and fruity.

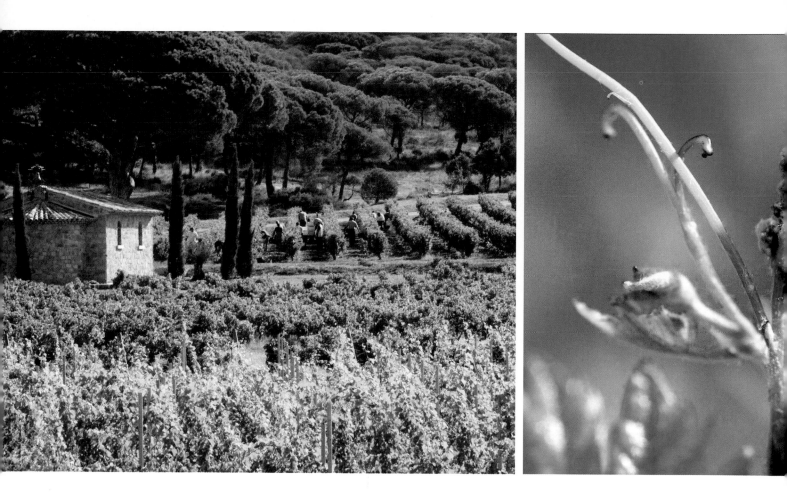

GETTING TO KNOW THE WINES OF PROVENCE MEANS GETTING to know the region itself—its history, traditions, and culture. In Provence, wine is inextricably linked to culture and lifestyle as part of Provence's *art de vivre*—the art of living that both locals and travelers alike seek.

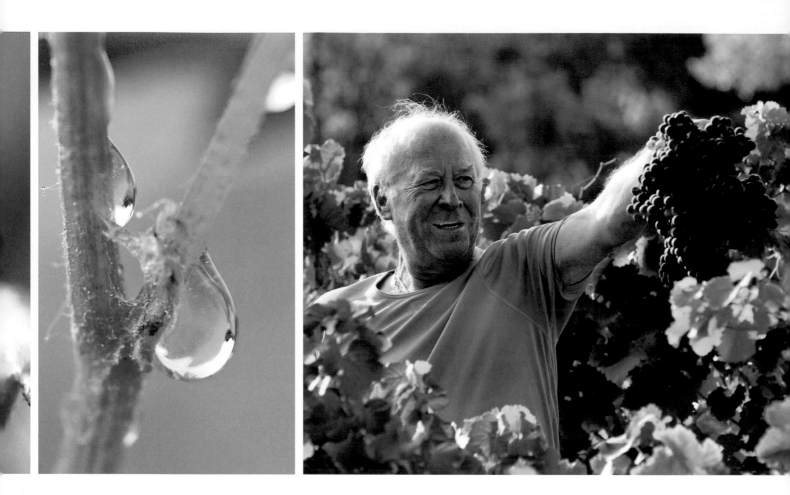

The vineyards of Provence extend from the Mediterranean in the south to the foothills of the Alps in the north; from Nice and the Riviera in the east to the dramatic landscapes of the Alpilles and Aix-en-Provence in the west. Each area is unique, with its own beauty and pleasures to explore.

The vintner's know-how is the product of centuries of patience and respect for nature.

HISTORY

The story of Provençal wine goes back more than 2,600 years. In 600 BCE, the Phocaeans, Greek sailors from Asia Minor, landed on the coast of Provence and founded Massalia (modern-day Marseille, Provence's largest city). The Phocaeans brought with them a new plant, the grapevine, and established the

very first French vineyards. The wine they made there was rosé. With that, French winemaking was born.

In the second century BCE, the Romans arrived and established an identity for the area as La Provincia Romana, the foundation of present-day Provence. They built the military port of Forum Julii (known today as Fréjus), where Roman ruins still dot the landscape, and the town of Aquae Sextiae (present-day Aix-en-Provence). The Romans ensured that the culture of grape growing and winemaking flourished.

The vine traveled north, taking root in the Rhône valley, Beaujolais, Burgundy, Gascony, and Bordeaux, some of France's most famous wine regions. But sunny Provence is where it all began.

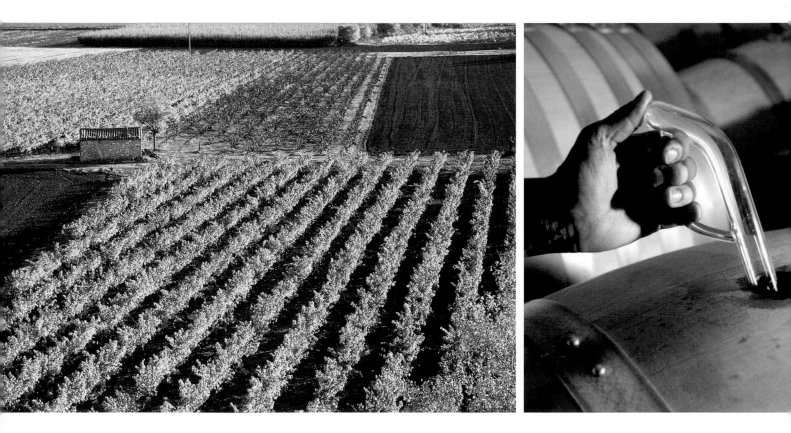

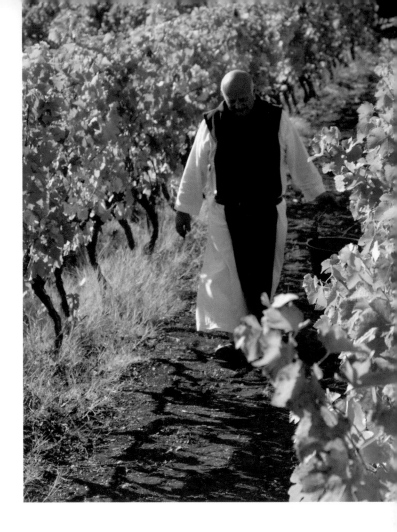

After the fall of Rome, Barbarian tribes ravaged Provence, as they did most of Europe. These were difficult times for the vineyards. The grapevines were neglected and didn't recover until the Middle Ages, when strong monastic orders revived them and further developed wine cultivation. Through donations from rich families, the monasteries increased their land holdings and became important economic powers. Between the fifth and twelfth centuries, monks made wine not only for their own use and for holy masses, but also to sell for profit, thus initiating the wine trade.

In the fourteenth century, grape and wine production expanded beyond monasteries. Noble families, royals, and high-ranking army officers acquired and developed vineyards, laying the foundation of today's wine industry in Provence.

In the beginning, wine was light in color, close to today's rosé (this type of wine has been known for centuries in the English-speaking world as *clairet*, wines made from red grapes that are very pale in color). From ancient engravings, we know that the grapes were pressed immediately after being picked, leaving almost no time for the juice to be in contact with the grape skins (which is how wine gets its color).

Through the Middle Ages, wines remained light in color, and the palest wines were prized by royals and nobles. These first wines also tasted nothing like wines today: to preserve them, winemakers often added spices, herbs, resin, and honey. Gradually, as tastes changed and it became easier to make and age wine, red wines became more sought after. Today, Provence makes white, red, and rosé wines, but the birthplace of French wine still focuses on the tradition of making rosé.

THIS PAGE: For centuries, monastic orders have advanced viticulture.

OPPOSITE PAGE: Fall descends like a rust-colored blanket over the countryside; meanwhile, the cellar master teaches students about wine.

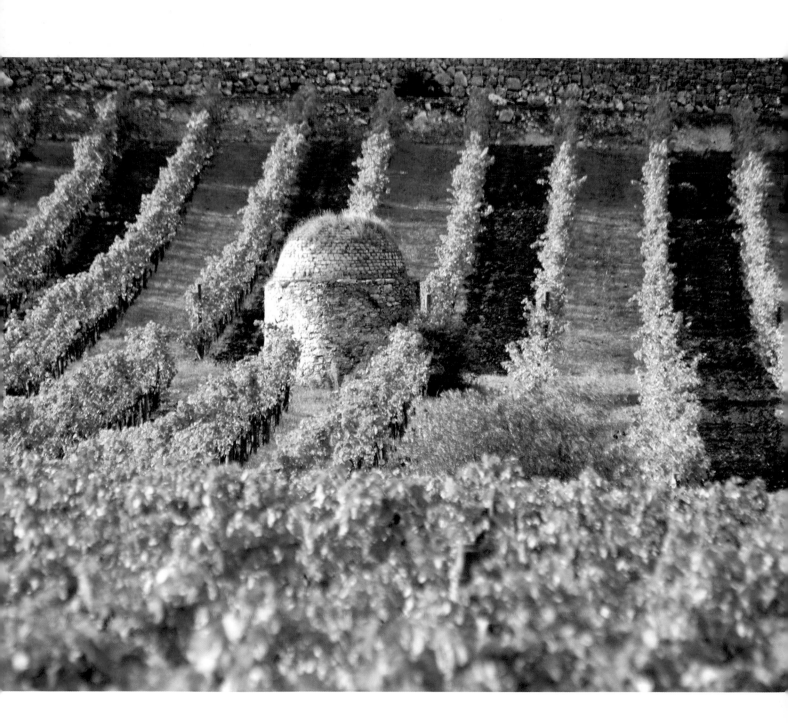

In the late eighteenth century, all of France (and most of Europe) experienced the devastating effects of the phylloxera, an aphid native to North America that over a couple of decades destroyed many French vineyards, including several in Provence. It was a time of crisis. When a solution was finally found (grafting French vines onto American rootstock, which was naturally immune), French grape growers were able to revive their vineyards after much effort and investment.

The start of the twentieth century brought new crises: for example, overproduction led to a sharp drop in prices. At this point, the first cooperatives emerged as grape growers sought to combine their resources to better approach the market. At the same time, the first grape-growing and winemaking controls were established to regulate the surface area under vines, the quality of the product, and the vines' yields. Gradually, other layers of regulation were added, including assurances that a wine was produced in a certain area. French wine law, which to this day regulates all wine production in France, emerged partly in response to a phylloxera epidemic and the resulting overproduction of French vineyards in the early twentieth century.

In 1935, the governing body of wine law, the Institut National des Appellations d'Origine (INAO), was formed. INAO's role was to specify the areas where certain wines could be produced and define the rules of production. Thus, the French system of *Appellation d'Origine Contrôlée* (AOC) was born. An AOC is a delineated zone of production (a region, subregion, village, or even a plot of land) that has unique qualities due to its geography, climate, soils, and grape-growing and winemaking practices. It is the highest point in the French wine quality pyramid.

The first AOCs were awarded to areas of historical significance for wine production—areas that were not only unique, but had also been producing quality wines for a long time. One of the first AOCs was in Provence—the historical AOC of Cassis, a dot of land overlooking steep hills that drop straight into the Mediterranean. Later, Provence received eight more AOCs, as more of its wine-producing areas were recognized for their quality.

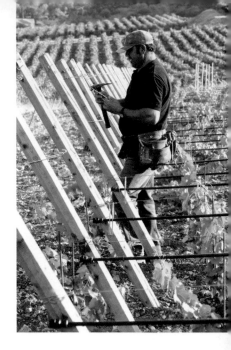

Provence is dotted with remnants of its past. Techniques have evolved, but certain nods to tradition remain.

PROVENCE *TERROIR*

Terroir can seem like an esoteric concept that's often used but rarely explained. It is simply the interplay of geology (soils and subsoils), geography, climate, and human know-how. Soils, geography, and climate largely determine what grapes can be planted in an area and what styles of wine can be produced. And in Provence's diverse geology, geography, and climate, *terroir* provides many unique expressions in its wines.

The north of Provence is dominated by hills and rocky outcrops sculpted by centuries of erosion. Sainte-Victoire and Sainte-Baume, mountains made of limestone, and the Gorges du Verdon, a river canyon, shape the landscape in powerful ways, and the higher elevation and wind protection from the mountains affect the climate, creating a cooler, more stable environment. These limestone hills are covered with *garrigue*—a fragrant Mediterranean scrub made up of lavender, rosemary, thyme, and other aromatic herbs—which gives an unmistakable, seductive smell to the entire area.

In the east, close to the sea, the hills are softer, with gentle slopes covered in Mediterranean shrub. The soil is primarily composed of crystalline rock in the Maures and Tanneron. Still further east, between Saint-Tropez and Cannes, the crystalline rock is broken up by ancient volcanic eruptions, which created the colorful Estérel massif (mountain range). *Maquis*, a dense Mediterranean shrub, covers the crystalline soils of this eastern coastal area.

The soils in Provence are nutrient-poor yet well drained, which makes them a perfect home for the grapevine, the ultimate Mediterranean plant. The lack of organic matter suppresses aggressive vegetative growth and prevents high yields—which, surprisingly, are good things. The vine has to struggle in these soils, but that struggle leads to wines with flavor, personality, and impact.

Provence gets an average of 2,700 to 3,000 hours of sunshine a year. The summers are dry and hot, and most of the rain comes in the fall and spring. These are perfect growing conditions for the sun-loving grapevine, which matures there easily and without much threat of disease. The diversity of the landscape, however, creates variations in the climate; the hilly terrain, for example, causes pockets of warmer or cooler weather. And the famous *Mistral*,

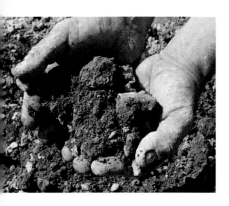

THIS PAGE: Provence's dry soil is ideal for winemaking.

OPPOSITE PAGE: Because of the hilly terrain, Provençal vineyards are often grown in terraces.

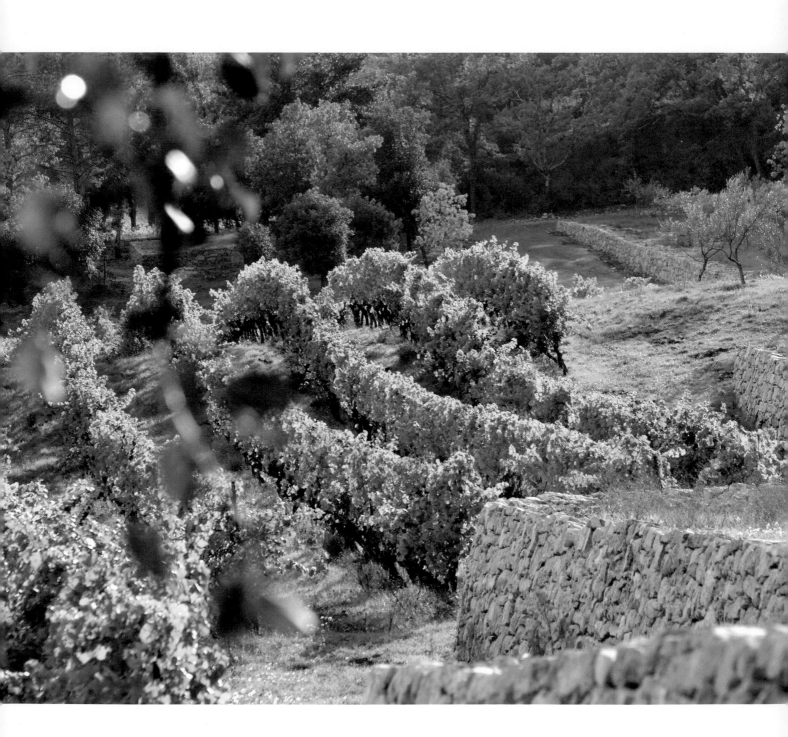

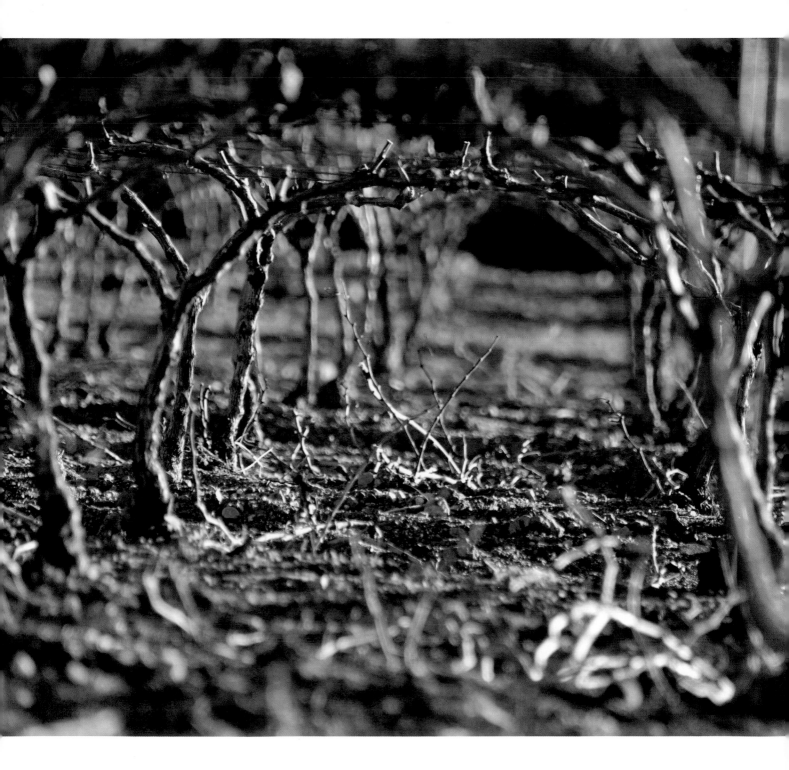

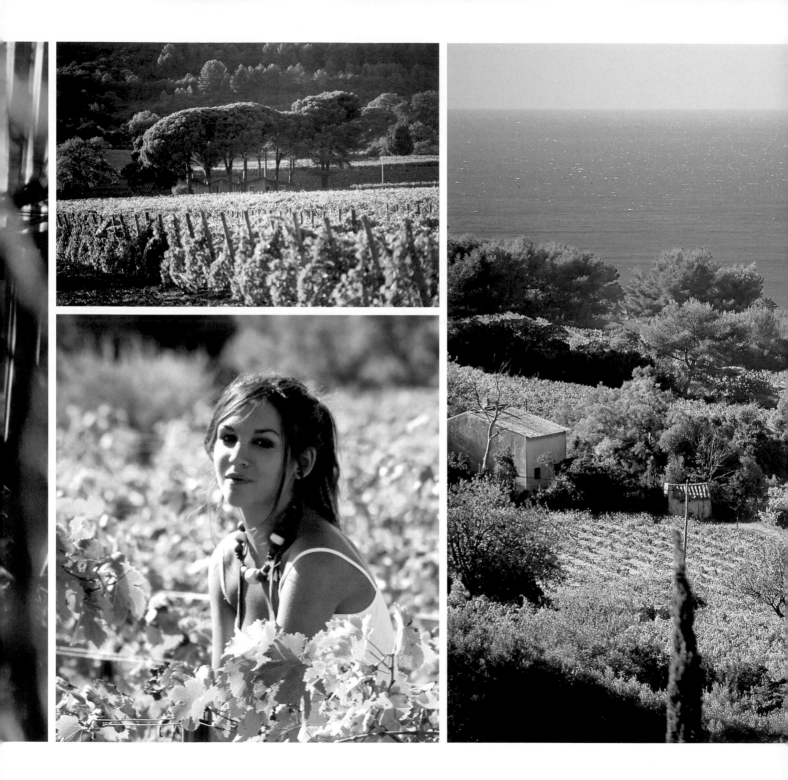

a strong northern wind that brings in cold air and dries the vines after rain, prevents diseases and mold.

All of this variety gives Provençal vintners the opportunity to craft many interesting wines, from crisp and fresh whites to flavorful dry rosés to memorable reds. The grapes used to make white wines include vermentino (called "rolle" in Provence), ugni blanc, clairette, sémillion, and bourboulenc blanc.

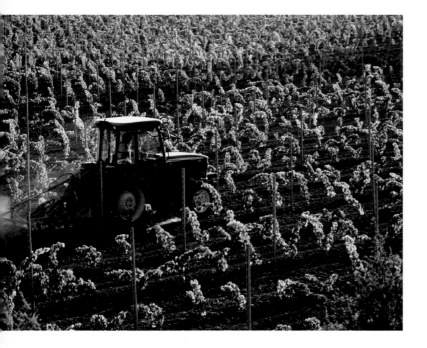

The reds and rosés are generally made from syrah, grenache, cinsault, tibouren, mourvédre, carignan, and cabernet sauvignon grapes. Some of these grapes grow throughout the region, and others thrive in small areas with specific microclimates. Whether well known and common or unique and relatively obscure, in the hands of skilled winemakers these grapes give expression to the *terroirs* of Provence.

For 26 centuries, Provençal winemakers have worked with nature, respecting her gifts and remembering that each vintage is different. The vine is an ever-changing, living thing and the best winemakers use that to their benefit, creating wines that express the unique nature of the grape and the features of the *terroir*. The grape varieties are picked at different times, vinified separately to preserve the typical flavors and

The caliber of the wine depends primarily on the quality of the grape.

aromas, and then blended. The blend varies from year to year, depending on the qualities of the vintage, but the aim is always to produce a harmonious, pleasant wine that expresses the individuality of the grape and the particulars of the vintage. The vintner is like an orchestra conductor, creating harmony by skillfully giving expression to many different voices. It is a difficult task that requires much passion and dedication—two traits necessary for successful wine production in Provence.

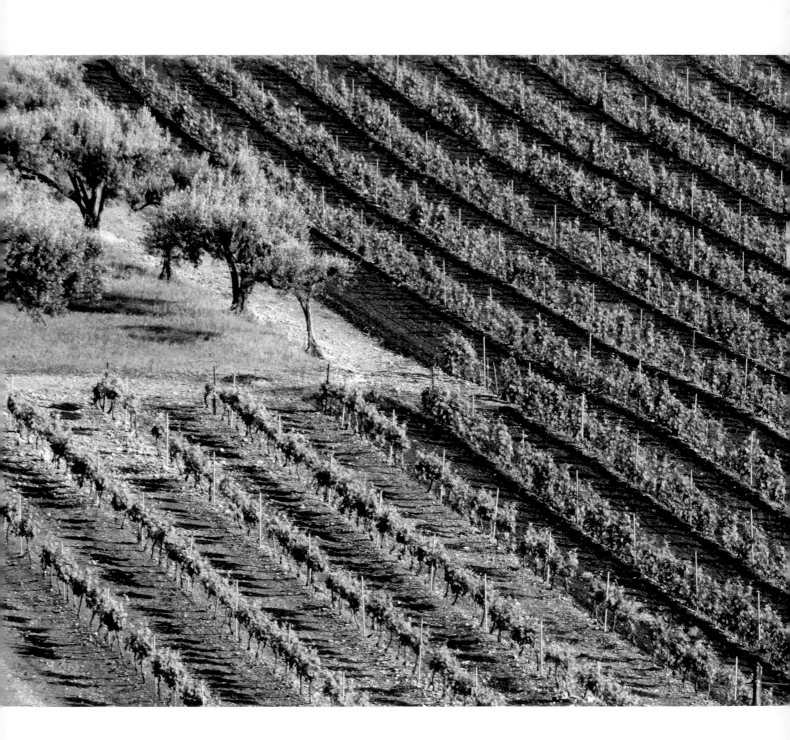

PROVENCE AOCS

The extraordinary diversity of Provençal soils, geography, and climate gives rise to wines that express the unique characteristics of the areas where the grapes are grown. This concept is captured in a wine's AOC certification. AOCs identify the area where certain grapes can be grown, regulate how those grapes are to be treated, and define how the wines will be made.

Provence has nine AOCs, but its three largest—Côtes de Provence, Coteaux d'Aix-en-Provence, and Coteaux Varois en Provence—account for about 96 percent of the volume of all AOC wine produced in Provence. These three large AOCs have united to form the Conseil Interprofessionnel des Vins de Provence (CIVP), which provides research and technical expertise, increases awareness of Provence wines, and highlights the unique qualities of each appellation and *terroir*.

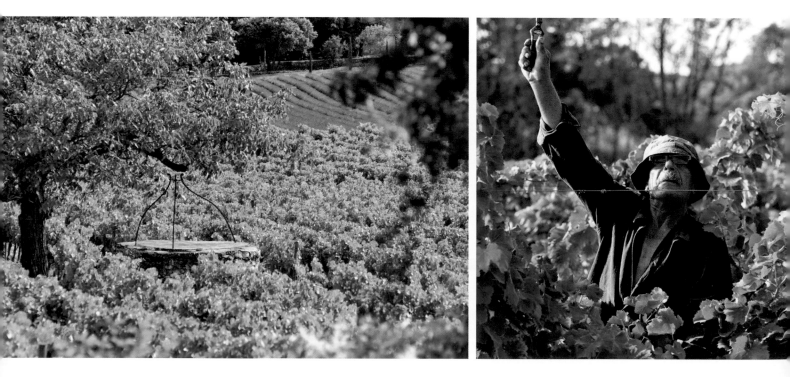

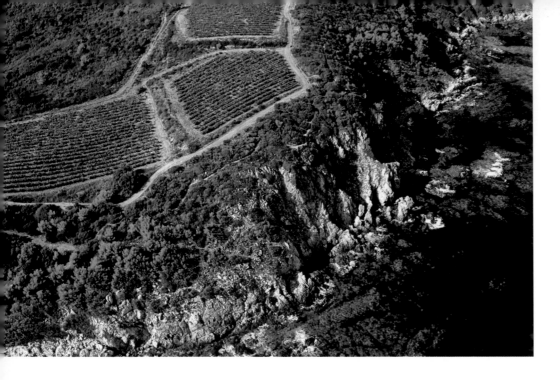

From the crystalline ridges by the sea to the limestone hills farther inland, Provence's geography is as diverse and unique as its inhabitants.

Côtes de Provence

Côtes de Provence, Provence's largest AOC, stretches from seaside vineyards to inland valleys to the hills of Saint-Victoire. The area has diverse soils, from the limestone hills of the northwest to the crystalline soils of the southeast. There are multiple subregions, each with unique soils and climate. Most of the wine produced in Côtes de Provence is rosé.

The vineyards in the north of the appellation (Haute Provence) spread across a landscape of hills and valleys with red, iron-rich earth and Mediterranean vegetation. The grapevine here resembles the strong and tenacious *garrigue* with which it shares space. This is a little-known area of Provence, with small mountain villages clinging to the rock and a landscape that surprises the traveler.

Farther south, to the north of the Maures massif, erosion has created a croissant-shaped depression where the soils are crystalline on one side and limestone on the other. Still farther south, the Maures and Estérel rock masses are mostly crystalline, albeit interspersed with volcanic rocks from long-ago eruptions.

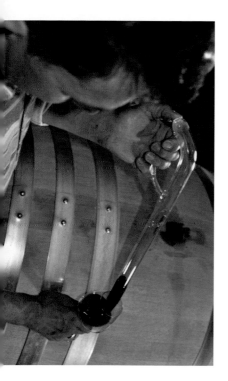

Because of this diversity, and because of the length of time it takes for these *terroirs* to be recognized legally, the Côtes de Provence AOC is still in the process of defining its *terroirs*. To date, four sub-AOCs, or *terroir* appellations, have been recognized: Sainte-Victoire, Fréjus, La Londe, and Pierrefeu. More are in the process of being defined.

It makes sense to think of the wines from this large area as a family of wines, *vins de Provence*. Under this family name, the different subzones can use their "first name," the name of the small area in which they are produced. And, as with people, all that is necessary to identify an area close to home is the first name (e.g., La Londe). The farther away one moves from home, the more necessary the last name (i.e., *vins de Provence)* becomes. That way, consumers can easily identify the general area, but also have a sense of where in that larger area the wines are from. These sub-AOCs are:

- ❖ *Côtes de Provence Sainte-Victoire.* This region is located east of Aix-en-Provence, at the foot of Mont Sainte-Victoire, the mountain that seduced Cézanne. This *terroir* appellation has a more continental climate. The mountains shelter it both from Mediterranean influences and from the northerly *Mistral,* creating a unique microclimate. This microclimate, combined with the area's nutrient-poor, well-drained soils consisting mostly of limestone and sandstone, enable the production of high-quality, memorable wines. The reds are powerful but silky, and the rosés are aromatic and elegant. The wines have an unmistakable mineral quality that recalls the limestone rocks of Sainte-Victoire.

- ❖ *Côtes de Provence Fréjus.* Between the red rocks of the Maures and Estérel massifs, where a little valley opens up, the Romans built their main war port in present-day Fréjus. Even that far back, the wines of this area were well known. Today, vines still thrive here in the land's crystalline soils and benefit from the climate, which is strongly influenced by the Mediterranean Sea. The rosés of Fréjus are aromatic, elegant, well rounded, and zesty on the palate.

- ❖ *Côtes de Provence La Londe.* In the vicinity of Hyères, the Maures massif veers away from the sea, leaving space for vineyards generously

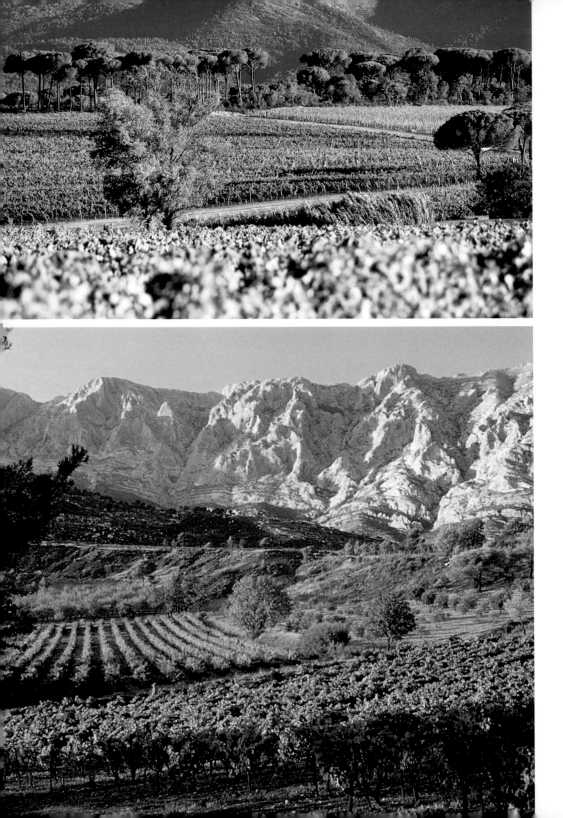

Fréjus and its
umbrella-like pines;
Sainte-Victoire
Mountain, whose soil
is excellent for red
wine cultivation.

THIS PAGE: In the appellation of La Londe, the vineyards slide right into the sea.

OPPOSITE PAGE: Aix-en-Provence, city of many fountains, is surrounded by several large wineries.

drenched in sun and Mediterranean Sea breezes. The vines send their roots through ancient crystalline soils and grow happily in a landscape that includes palm trees and mimosas caressed by maritime winds. This *terroir* appellation includes the picturesque island of Porquerolles, home to some of the most isolated vineyards in France. Here, overlooking the sandy beaches, the vines thrive close to the sea in a crystalline, rock-based soil called schist. These island wines are mineral and saline, tasting of the sea. The vineyards around Saint-Tropez—one of the most famous travel destinations in France—are also part of this sub-AOC. La Londe wines are elegant and distinctive, like the land on which the grapes grow.

❖ *Côtes de Provence Pierrefeu.* This most recent *terroir* appellation was recognized by INAO in November 2012 and first appeared on bottles with the 2013 harvest. Côtes de Provence Pierrefeu extends just to the west of Côtes de Provence La Londe, and stretches inland from the coast. It

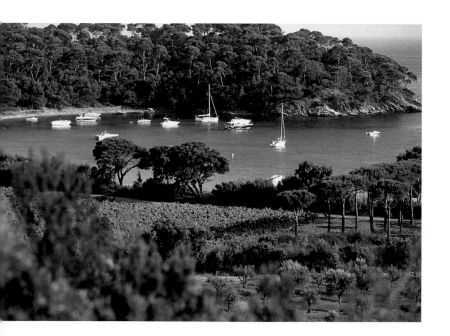

is responsible for 22 percent of all AOC Côtes de Provence production. This *terroir* appellation benefits from a Mediterranean influence and has a milder climate, with higher spring and summer temperatures, that enables the grapes to ripen easily and to do so earlier in the season. The area includes red, iron-rich, and sandy clay soils as well as stones that absorb heat during the day and radiate it back to the grapevines in the evening hours. The schist on the hillsides lends a particularly mineral character to the wines, which in turn express the character of the area. Both the reds and the rosés are distinctive, boasting plenty of personality and unique mineral qualities.

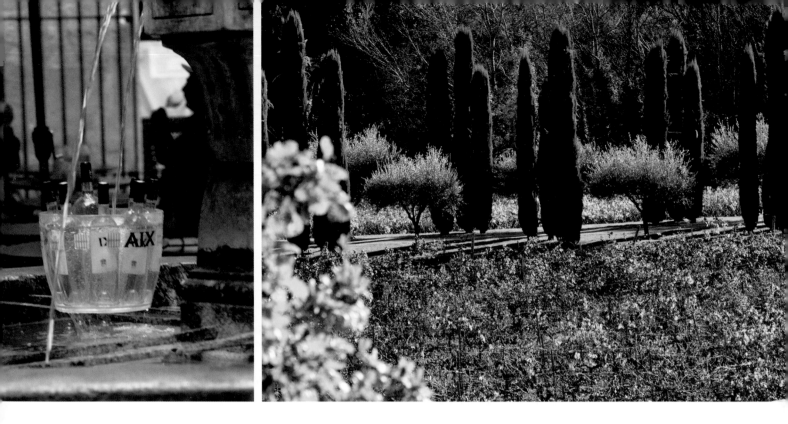

Coteaux d'Aix-en-Provence

Aix-en-Provence, the historic capital of Provence, is a city known for its water, fountains, and art—and also its wine. Surrounded by vineyards, it lends its name to the second-largest AOC in Provence: Coteaux d'Aix-en-Provence, which covers the west part of Provence and has mostly limestone soils (though the soils do vary greatly from north to south).

Most winemaking in Coteaux d'Aix-en-Provence is focused in the sedimentary basins between the mountain ranges that run parallel to the coast, from east to west. The *Mistral* plays an important role here: violent at times, it helps dry the leaves of the vines, preventing disease. Sun, *Mistral* winds, and limestone are the key elements of this AOC's *terroir*, creating perfect conditions for high-quality wines. Since the 1980s, the vineyards have evolved, using more modern production methods, and today an array of grape varieties produce interesting wines of all three colors (white, red, and rosé). The rosés are lively and bright pink, seducing the senses from the very first sip.

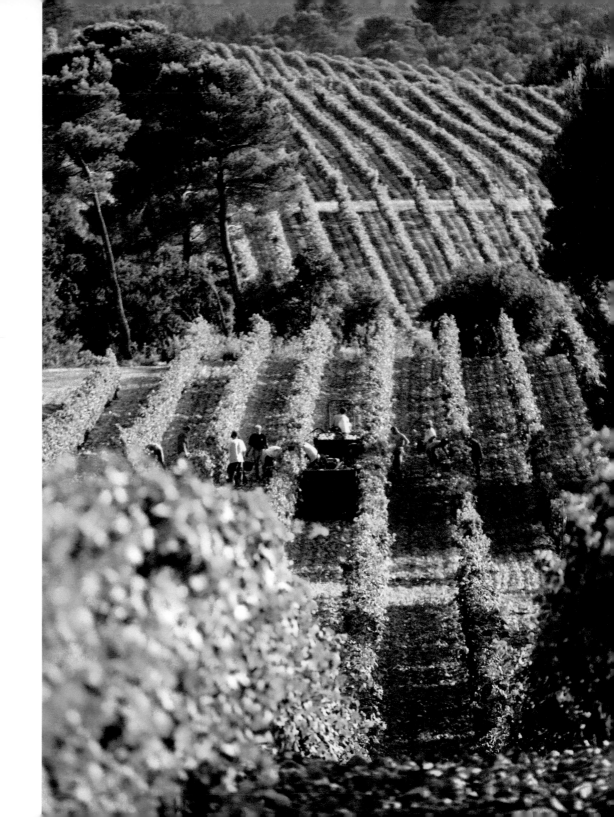

Coteaux Varois en Provence

Coteaux Varois en Provence lies between the largest portion of Côtes de Provence and Coteaux d'Aix-en-Provence. This is the true interior of Provence; because the landscape is so mountainous, the sea's influence doesn't reach it. Thus, Coteaux Varois has a more continental climate, with distinct seasons, hot summers, and cold winters. The climate, altitude (on average, about 1,200 feet above sea level), and unique geology of the clay and limestone hills cause the rosés of Coteaux Varois to be fuller bodied and more structured than those of other AOCs. Coteaux Varois also produces white and red wines.

Bandol

The terraced vineyards of Bandol, first planted by the Romans, still bask in the sun and the gentle sea breezes that give this AOC its special climate. The vineyards are planted in an amphitheater-style arrangement, opening up to the south and giving the grapes beneficial exposure to the sun. They are supported by manmade stone walls, and the soils in these vineyards are dry sandstone, marl, and limestone.

The mourvèdre grape, which must grow near the sea in order to thrive, has found a spiritual home here, and it produces reds and rosés of great character and distinction. Bandol also produces small amounts of fresh and crisp whites. The AOC rules of this historic appellation, which were established in 1941, are particularly strict and mandate green harvesting, low yields, and aging (in the case of the reds). These rules, combined with the exceptional *terroir*, produce excellent wines and place Bandol among the more sought-after AOCs in both domestic and international markets.

Cassis

Provence's oldest AOC, Cassis, is an exceptional place. The little village that gives the AOC its name is picturesque and animated. Tourists visit year-round, from near and far, to enjoy a glass of the AOC's celebrated white wine, take in the breathtaking views of the Mediterranean, or play a game of *pétanque*.

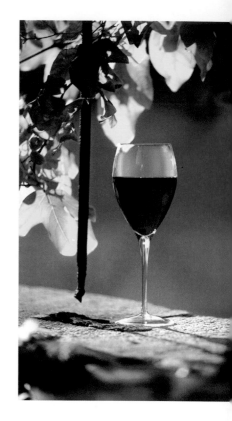

The clay and limestone hills of northern Provence are conducive to the production of high-quality red wine.

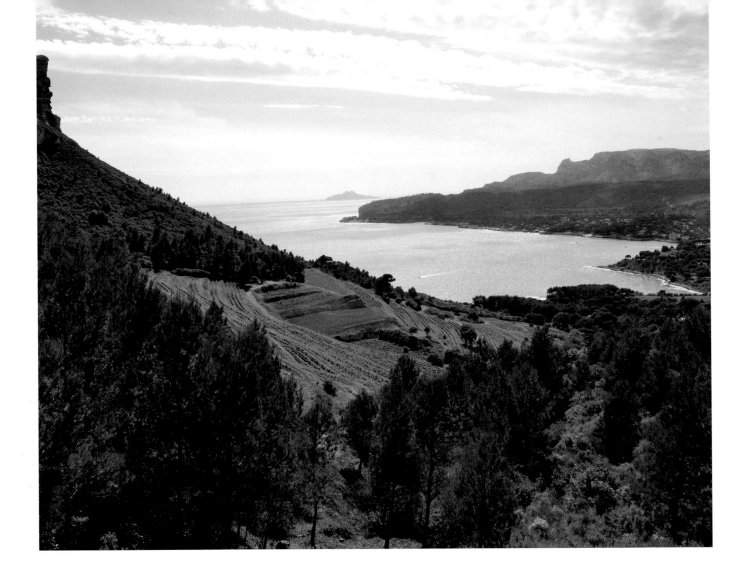

In Cassis, terraced vineyards are nestled on a cliff overlooking the Mediterranean.

The terraced vineyards are sandwiched between the village and deep, creviced limestone hills (called *calanques)* that rise nearby, sheltering them from the *Mistral.* The region's abundant sunshine and favorable sea breezes create perfect conditions for maturing healthy grapes.

Cassis is the only AOC in Provence where most of the wine produced is white. Its wines, based mostly on clairette and marsanne grapes, are complex and full of character, with floral and fruity notes. Cassis rosés are pale, elegant, and full of finesse.

Bellet

Only a short distance from Nice, Bellet's terraced vineyards claim what little land is available. Its grapes bask in the warm Mediterranean sun and cooling winds from the sea. This small AOC includes many unique grape varieties that combine to produce wines of character, with typical floral and citrus aromas and flavors.

Palette

Palette, the smallest AOC in Provence, has a unique micro-climate. Protected from northern winds by a circle of steep limestone hills but caressed by the western breezes that blow up the Arc River valley, Palette enjoys moderate weather in which many unusual grape varieties can flourish. The region's red, white, and rosé wines are aged in oak and destined for longevity.

Les Baux-de-Provence

Les Baux-de-Provence lies west of Coteaux d'Aix, on both sides of the Alpilles Mountains. The elevation (about 800 feet above sea level) and the dry and hot climate make Les Baux-de-Provence a stronghold of organic and biodynamic viticulture. The limestone soils and good growing conditions make this area perfect for producing high-quality wines. About ⅔ of the wine produced here is red, and the rest is rosé.

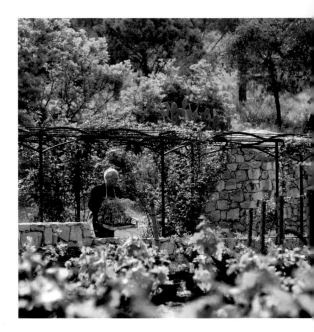

Pierrevert

This is Provence's newest and northernmost AOC. On the hillsides of northern Provence, the vines share space with the lavender fields of Haute Provence, which have become famous thanks to the efforts of countless writers, painters, and photographers. The high altitude (about 1,500 feet above sea level) and the region's nutrient-poor, well-drained soils produce well-structured reds and rosés and crisp whites.

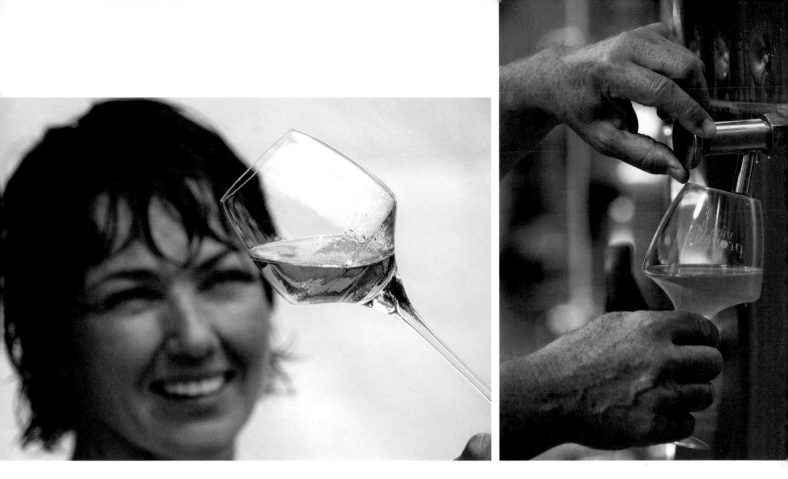

ROSÉ WINEMAKING

Provençal winemaking's
secrets yield wines that
are both bright and
fragrant.

Rosé is a difficult wine to make. Its pale, delicate color and fresh aromas require an attentive and skilled winemaker. Time is also of the essence, as vintners must make quick decisions throughout the process, from the time the grapes are harvested to the moment the wines are released. Extracting flavor and retaining the characteristic pale color of Provence rosé is a delicate process that requires care, vigilance, and the occasional sleepless night.

The pigments that give a wine its color are concentrated in the skins of the grapes. The pulp of most red grapes is colorless, so a wine's color depends on how long the grape's skin is left in contact with the juice—in other words, color depends on the amount of time the skins *macerate*. Red and rosé wines are made with red grapes, but rosés are lighter because the grapes macerate for

less time. Rosé's color also depends on the types of grapes used, the temperature at which the grapes grow, and the wine's vintage, as these factors vary from year to year. Different grapes contain different amounts of anthocyanins, the substances in grape skins that give them color, so making Provence rosé involves respecting the unique nature of each grape, knowing what the grape is capable of, and knowing how to treat it in order to achieve the best results. Thus, it takes a skilled vintner to produce quality rosé.

Traditionally, Provence rosés are produced using the press method, where the grapes are pressed immediately after being picked in order to minimize skin contact. Rosés made using this method are pale and preserve the freshness and aromas of the grapes. A second way to make rosé is the maceration method, where the grapes are crushed and the juice is left in contact with the skins for several hours at low temperatures. When the desired color and aromas have been achieved, the juice is removed and fermented as rosé.

The *saignée*, or "bleeding," method of making rosé, which is common in other regions, is relatively rare in Provence. In that method, only a part of the juice is drained after being in contact with the skins long enough to extract their flavor and aroma. The juice and skins that remain after *saignée* are then pressed to make red wine. Thus, in this method, rosé is a byproduct of red wine production, rather than the primary goal of the winemaker. In the press and maceration methods, all decisions are made with an eye toward producing top-quality rosé, yielding delicate, fresh aromas and pale, beautiful colors.

Fermenting rosé at low temperatures helps preserve the wine's freshness and aroma. The wine is stored between 60°F and 68°F (16°C to 20°C) in stainless steel tanks or lined cement vats. If the winemaker is looking to add richness and a rounder mouthfeel, rosés are aged on the *lees,* which are the yeasts used during fermentation. A few are aged in barrels, which produces even richer, fuller-bodied rosés that mature well.

Depending on which grapes are used and how the wine was made, the Provence rosé you're sipping might be one of six colors: gooseberry, peach, grapefruit, cantaloupe, mango, or mandarin. There are many different styles and shades of rosé in Provence, which makes exploring these wines a real pleasure for all the senses.

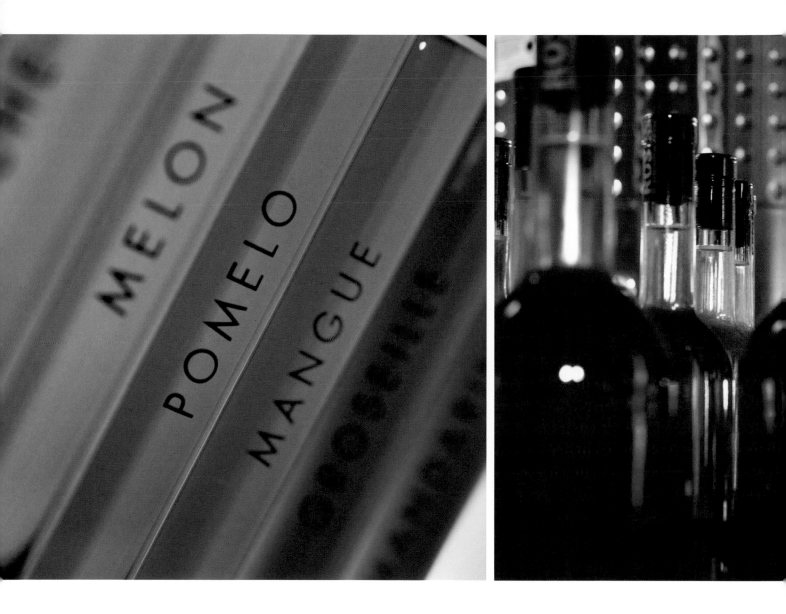

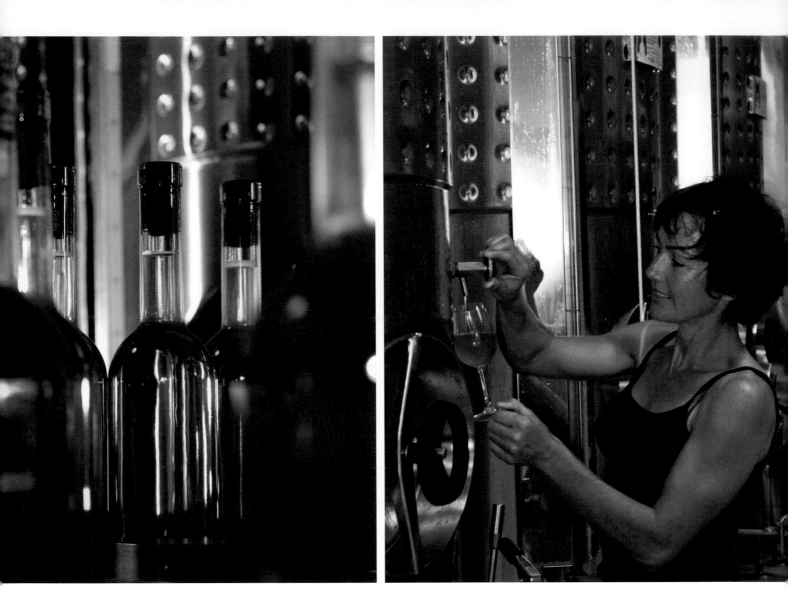

It takes a full year
of attentive care to
produce a dry, light,
and aromatic rosé.

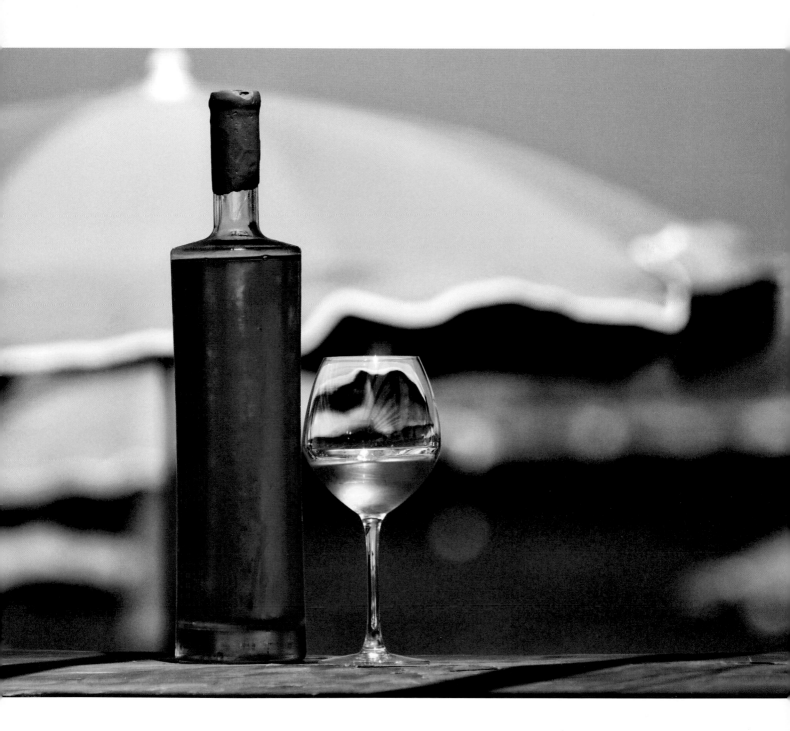

Enjoying Provence Rosé

Whether you're a seasoned wine drinker or just starting to explore the fascinating world of wine, tasting Provence rosé is a unique sensory experience. It is pleasurable, joyful, and full of surprises—elegant, aromatic, and dry yet fruity, these wines will seduce you from the first sip. So, practice the Provençal art of living, and remember, all that matters is whether you like a wine. Provence rosés are easy to love.

For the best tasting experience, start with a large, delicate, and clean glass. Pour in a measure of wine stored at just the right temperature (46°F to 53°F [8°C to 12°C]). Then, leave the technical details behind and give in to your senses. The color of a Provence rosé first excites the eye. Observe its pale and nuanced color, pure and brilliant, calling to mind sunshine and clear blue skies.

Next, inhale its tantalizing aromas: floral, fruity, and sometimes rich and tropical, but always fresh and inviting. Swirl the glass and continue exploring the layers of aromas that leap out. Resist tasting the wine, if you can, and instead immerse yourself in its aromas. Imagine the hills that grew the grapes, the sun that caressed them, and the hands that picked them.

When you cannot resist any more, take a small sip. Hold it on your tongue and let it sink into your taste buds. Swirl it gently, let it caress the edges of the palate; let it awaken your taste buds. Note how crisp and fresh the wine is. Flavors are perceived in layers, so take another sip and experience the wine's depth and richness. Each moment brings new and surprising tastes: fruit, but also minerals, and sometimes a salty note. As the wine glides through your mouth, the flavors strengthen, enveloping your senses and transporting you to the sunny place that created the wine. When finally you swallow, the flavors and aromas explode in the back of your mouth, uniting the senses of smell and taste. The experience is now complete and your thirst has been quenched, but the enjoyment is far from over.

Tasting rosé is all about pleasure, part of the quintessential Provençal art of living. Immerse yourself in it!

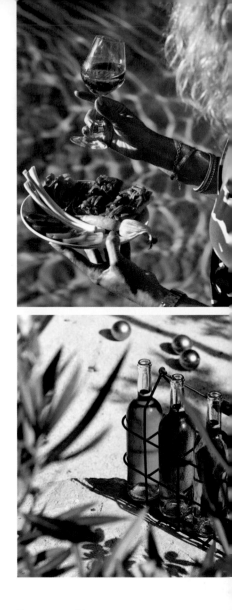

Provence rosé is a distinguished wine on its own, but it is also an integral part of the Provençal lifestyle.

THE WINES OF PROVENCE

Provence wines are inseparable from Provence food. Provençal cooks and winemakers are passionate about the aromas and tastes of their land and combining them to achieve extraordinary results. After all, the art of living is about pleasing the senses.

In Provence, rosé often ushers in the meal as a symbol of hospitality. To welcome friends and guests, Provençals immediately offer them a glass of rosé, signifying that the party is about to start.

Provence rosé can be matched with summer salads, goat cheese, and *ratatouille*, and it goes equally well with fish, mussels, and *bouillabaisse*. It's crisp and lively, the acidity perfectly balanced by a variety of flavors. It's dry, but with a pleasant fruitiness that matches many different foods.

Provence rosé is the perfect companion for all courses of a meal. It evokes Provence and the Mediterranean foods typical of its sunny region, but also matches perfectly with many ethnic dishes rich in spices and exotic flavors. It is the perfect complement to the modern lifestyle, where meals are lighter and less structured, often consisting of a single course.

With a balance of body, acidity, and flavor, rosé brings together the world of red and white wines into one perfect sip. Whether the occasion is an intimate dinner under the stars, a beach picnic, a rooftop party, or a simple family dinner, rosé is at ease in any environment.

This playful and cheery wine is also free of the formality generally associated with wine drinking. Rosé does not need decanters or special equipment—all you need is a well-chilled bottle. Unsurprisingly, rosé wows both red- and white-wine lovers. Whether as a companion to food or by itself as an aperitif in winter or summer (and in Provence or any other place in the world), rosé brings people together.

Remember, wine is a product of not just the earth, but also the people who work the land. Getting to know a wine isn't just about knowing the region it comes from. It's also about understanding the people who are able

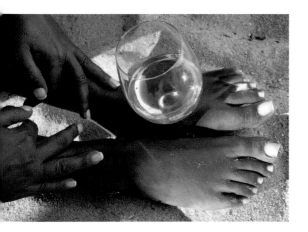

Although best known for rosé, the vineyards of Provence also produce fantastic red and white wines.

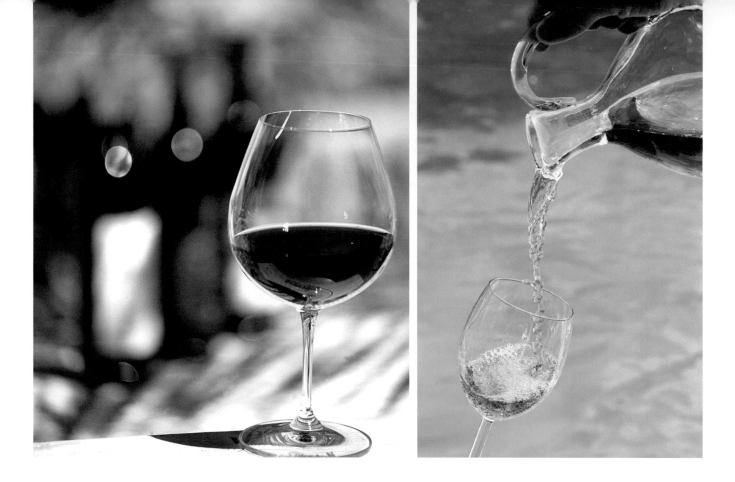

to transform their passion and knowledge into an enchanting glass of rosé. Each wine tells a story.

Rosé isn't the only wine Provence is famous for. Its white wines are fresh, crisp, well balanced, and full of flavor. Elegant, sophisticated, and complex, they can be barrel aged, acquiring added richness. They are perfect as an aperitif, with salads, and with fish and seafood, all staples of the region. Fuller-bodied whites enhance any white meat and even truffle dishes.

Provence reds can be young, fresh, and lively, or richer, lush, and velvety. The fruity young reds pair well with seafood and fish, enhance the flavors of Mediterranean herbs, and match the body of vegetable dishes. They are best when slightly chilled. Fuller-bodied reds, some of which are barrel aged for added complexity and structure, heighten the enjoyment of any meat dish and are often served at the end of the meal with aged cheeses.

ISLAND WINES

Wines made on islands are unique. Proximity to the sea imparts an unmistakable salinity and mineral quality to any wine, and the wines of Provençal islands are no exception. One sip of a wine from Porquerolles or Saint-Honorat drives the point home. These wines, whether they are red, white, or rosé, have a zesty minerality that gives them extraordinary length on the palate. You can taste the salt of the Mediterranean and the minerals drawn from the soils. Of course, these wines pair beautifully with seafood from the crystal blue waters that surround the islands.

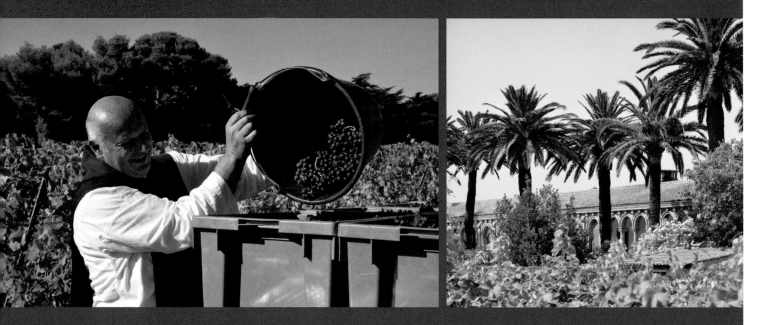

On the island of Saint-Honorat, the Abbaye de Lérins, a monastic community of 20, lives by the fruits of its labor. The community produces distinctive red and white wines.

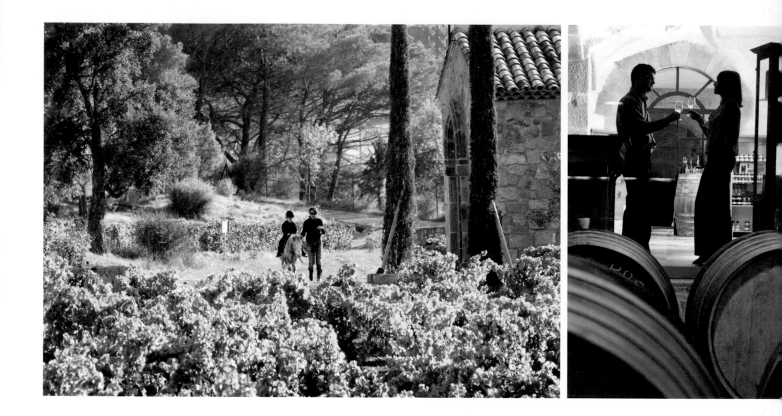

Wine Tourism

Visitors and locals alike can explore the regional wines and the many excellent vineyards of Provence though travel and tastings. After all, there is no better way to learn about a wine than by tasting it in its homeland and meeting the people who make it. Route des Vins de Provence, the oeno-gastronomy division of Provence's office of tourism, combines wine exploration with other cultural experiences, including art shows, music events, and food festivals.

Wine is a product of tradition, culture, land, passion, and effort, and it is wonderful to witness it all firsthand. From Nice to the Camargue, 350 wineries and cooperative cellars open their doors to visitors who seek a more personal experience and an opportunity to gain a deeper understanding of the culture and traditions of this rich land. Getting to each one of the wineries is itself a beauty-filled experience, the charming Provençal landscape ever changing and revealing its endless splendor.

You can't truly know a wine until you've met the person who made it.

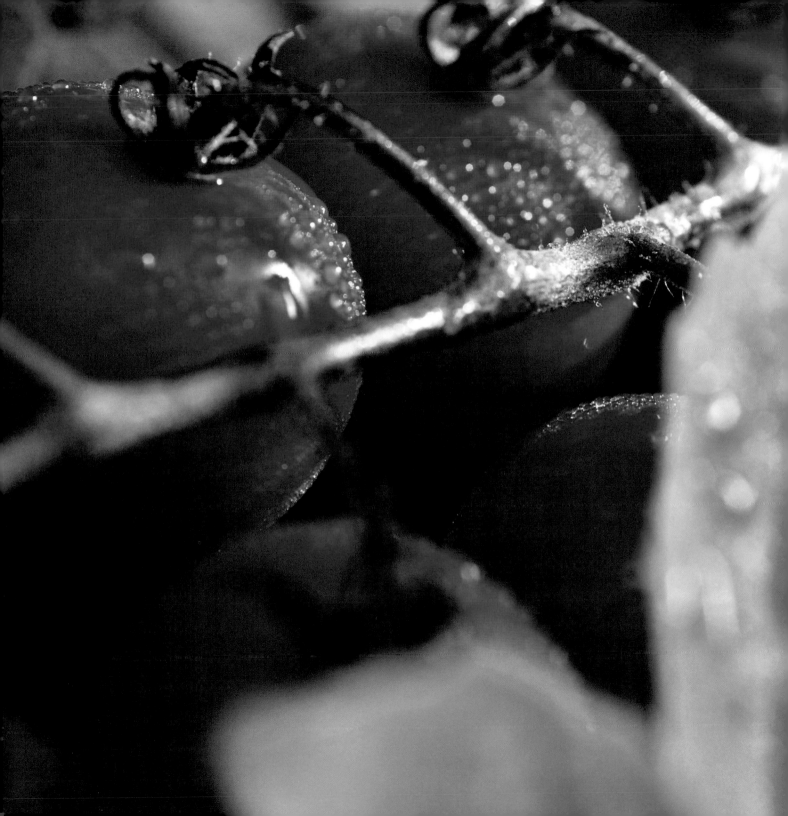

The Cuisine
of Provence

PROVENÇAL FOOD IS AT THE CORE OF WHAT IS KNOWN AS the Mediterranean diet. This diet has been the traditional way of eating in Provence for centuries—fruits, vegetables, extra virgin olive oil, nuts, and fish are in abundance here, so the Provençals devised countless creative recipes to make use of these riches. Research shows that this way of eating lowers the risk of heart disease and cancer and reduces the incidence of Parkinson and Alzheimer diseases.

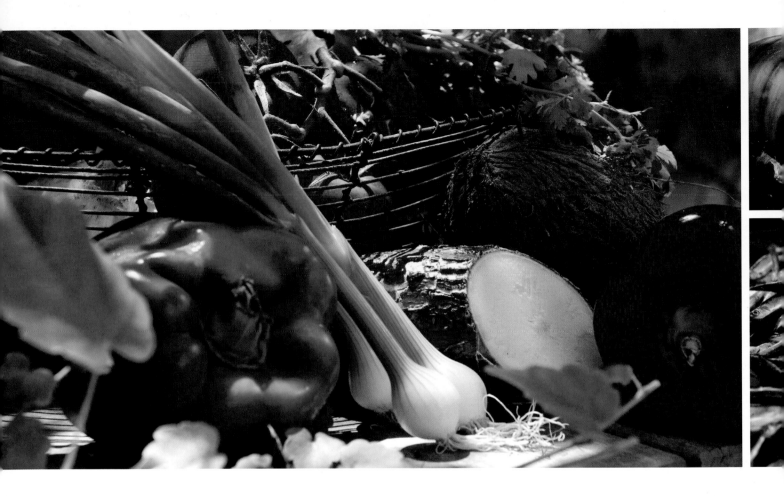

THE ENDURING CONNECTION TO THE FOODS THEY EAT IS JUST
one way Provençals celebrate life. Food is sustenance, but it's also art; it's a
creative process that involves all the senses. In Provençal cooking, the ingredients are always the stars of the show. As the recipes in this book will remind you,
each meal starts at the market. Provençal cooks might take a ripe tomato, an
eggplant, and some olive oil, and *voilà!*—a delicious and nutritious dish is born.

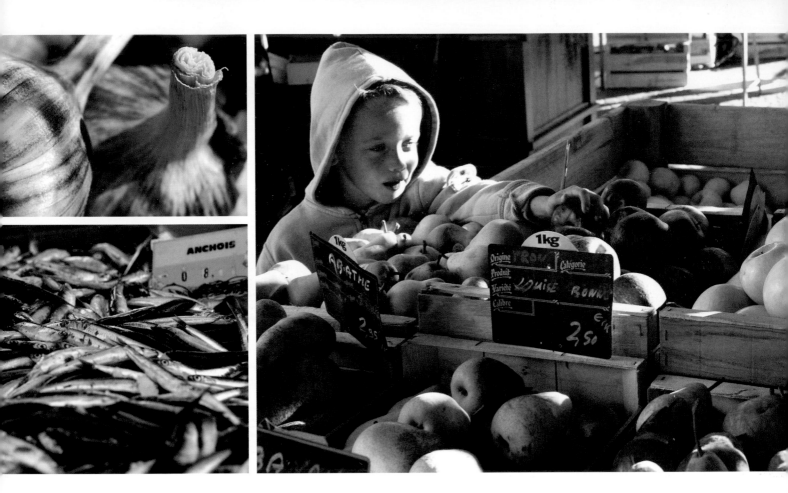

Because the ingredients are fresh and flavorful, the dishes are satisfying yet light. They are prepared simply, often grilled or roasted and seasoned with local herbs and spices. Vegetables and fish retain their freshness and great flavor when cooked this way. When cooked for a long time over low temperatures, good ingredients develop deeper, richer flavors, making each bite a morsel worth savoring.

In Provence, there is no strict division between the parts of a meal, unlike the cuisines of other French regions. Dishes such as *ratatouille* and *anchoïade*, for example, are not appetizers or main dishes. *Anchoïade* arrives at the table surrounded with all kinds of vegetables to be shared and enjoyed slowly with a glass of rosé.

The cuisine of Provence uses more vegetables and fish than that of any other French region. Red meat is not common in the everyday Provençal diet. Extra virgin olive oil is the basis for all dishes, whether they are prepared in restaurants or at home. This is the only region in France where vegetables are not a side dish, but instead are an essential part of the meal.

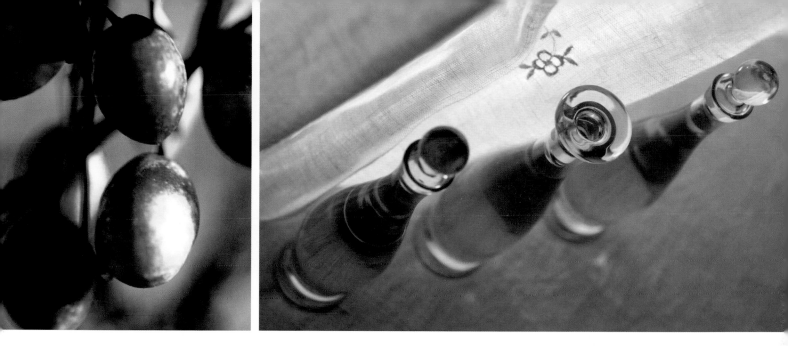

In Provence, the Mediterranean diet is more of a lifestyle: a glass of wine enjoyed with friends, relaxation in the sun, a game of *pétanque*, and plenty of good cheer. So, as you delight in the recipes in this book and explore Provence's zesty rosés, ease into the Mediterranean lifestyle, gather your friends, and smile. Practice *l'art de vivre!*

Olive Oil

The olive tree, long a symbol of Mediterranean civilization, is a fixture of the Provençal landscape—so much so that Provence's borders are often described as "where the olive trees end." The olive tree thrives in this sun-drenched land, and olives find their way into everything, from edible delicacies such as tapenade to medicines and famous Marseille soap (see p. 12).

Of course, Provençal cooks make great use of extra virgin olive oil. In addition to cooking with it, they also drizzle it on finished dishes to add flavor and complexity. In Provence, olive oil is similar to wine, in that its flavor and aromas vary widely depending on the variety of olive, the soil the tree is grown in, climate, geography, and the producer's know-how. Connoisseurs speak of olive oils the way wine lovers speak of fine wines: an oil might be lightly fruity

or spicy and peppery, and might have notes of artichoke, almond, green apple, freshly mown grass, or even chocolate.

Provençal oils range from light and subtle to assertive and peppery. Producers classify these oils into three broad categories:

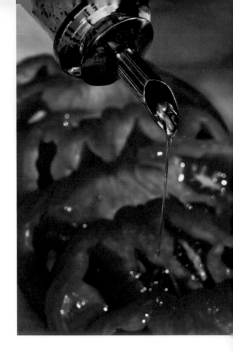

- Fruity green (*fruité vert*): These oils have a fresh, slightly peppery taste and aromas of fresh artichokes and tomato leaves. They're made from olives picked early, while still green, and processed within 24 hours.

- Fruity ripe (*fruité mûr*): This type of oil features aromas of berries, citrus, and almond. It's made from olives that are ripe, black, and processed immediately.

- Fruity black (*fruité noir*): This oil has the most assertive flavor of all. The olives are picked late, when they are fully ripe and bursting with flavor, and stored at the mill for several days before being processed. The resulting oil is sweet, with hints of mushroom, dried fruit, and even cocoa and chocolate. Fruity black olive oils are not classified as extra virgin; because the olives undergo carefully controlled fermentation, the oils must be classified as virgin. They do not have the same health benefits as extra virgin olive oils, but, used sparingly, they add incredible flavor to full-bodied dishes.

Just as wine pairs with food, so too does olive oil: lighter oils complement vegetables, salads, and raw or simply prepared fish, adding flavor and richness without overpowering the ingredients. They also pair well with young chèvre, basil sorbet, citrus salads, or perhaps poached peaches with a touch of mint.

More robust oils are perfect for finishing stronger-flavored fish, poultry, roasted rabbit, potatoes, chickpeas, fresh pasta, or risotto. The fruit component also makes them perfect complements to fruit-based desserts, including grilled pineapple with spices and olive oil ice cream.

Fruity black olive oils are perfect for any food with rich, concentrated flavors: slow-cooked lamb stew, *ratatouille*, aged chèvre, grilled peppers, mashed potatoes, quince, or pear compote and cooked apples.

Find yourself a reputable source of Provençal olive oil and delight your taste buds!

The Mediterranean diet isn't complete without the golden glint of a high-quality fruity olive oil.

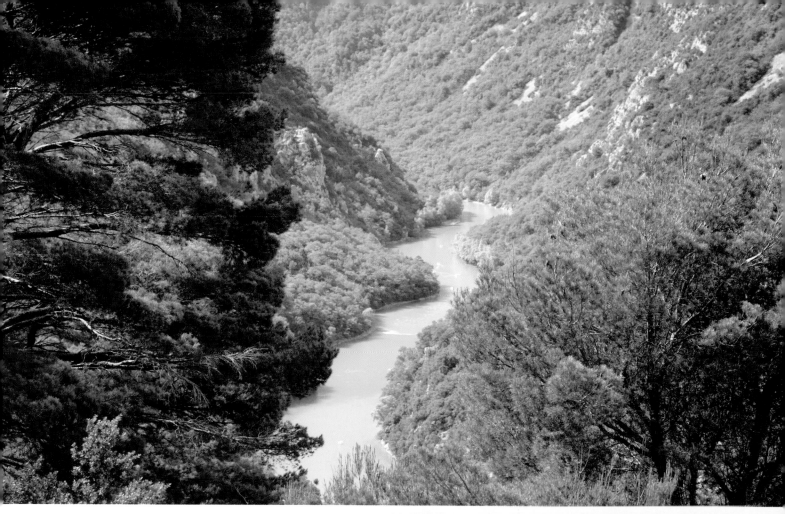

The road that runs along the breathtaking Gorges du Verdon affords incredible views of the steep bluish walls of the canyon and the river below, which is a milky green from the limestone it cuts through.

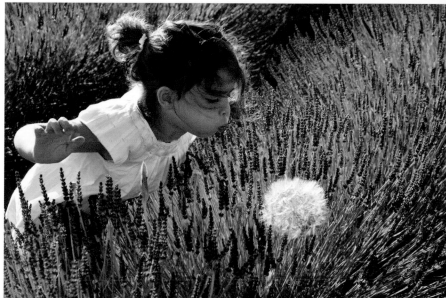

Aix-en-Provence and Haute Provence

TUCKED AWAY IN THE NORTH OF PROVENCE, SOME DISTANCE AWAY from the sunny beaches and palm trees, Haute Provence is as surprising as it is beautiful. Remote and rugged, with desert landscapes and deep canyons, it harbors fascinating traditions and captivates with its purity. Harsh winters, with strong, unrelenting winds, and hot, dry summers shape the landscape and local foods.

To the south lies the elegant city of Aix-en-Provence, which the Romans called the City of Water because of its many beautiful fountains. It is the historical capital of Provence. The city has a remarkable architectural heritage. Its narrow streets house incredible art, markets, artisanal stores, and many other attractions.

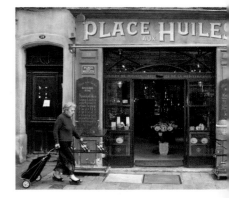

Aix and its urban sophistication aside, the beauty of Haute Provence can also be found in its many small mountain villages known for centuries-old traditions. For example, Moustiers-Sainte-Marie, one of the most beautiful villages in France, clings to a rock wall on the western edge of the Gorges du Verdon. Moustiers is famous for *faïence*, fine glazed pottery, and the studios and shops that line the steep streets of the town offer visitors a peek into the world of this artisanal tradition.

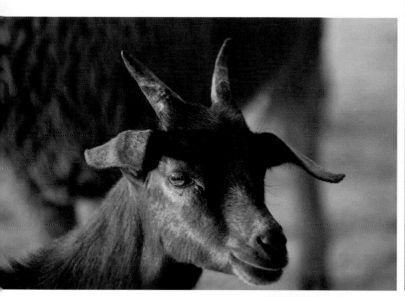

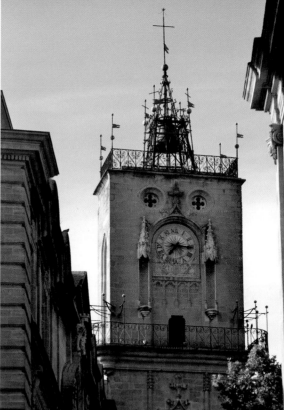

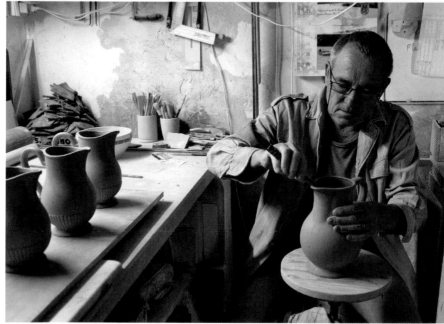

CLOCKWISE FROM TOP LEFT:
Mountain sheep and goats
skillfully scale the rocks
and find just enough
shrubbery and herbs to
survive; The clock tower
in the square in front of
Aix-en-Provence's *hôtel
de ville* (city hall); In
the spring and summer,
the fields are alive with
flowers, rosemary,
thyme, and juniper; An
artisanal *faïence* maker in
Moustiers-Sainte-Marie.

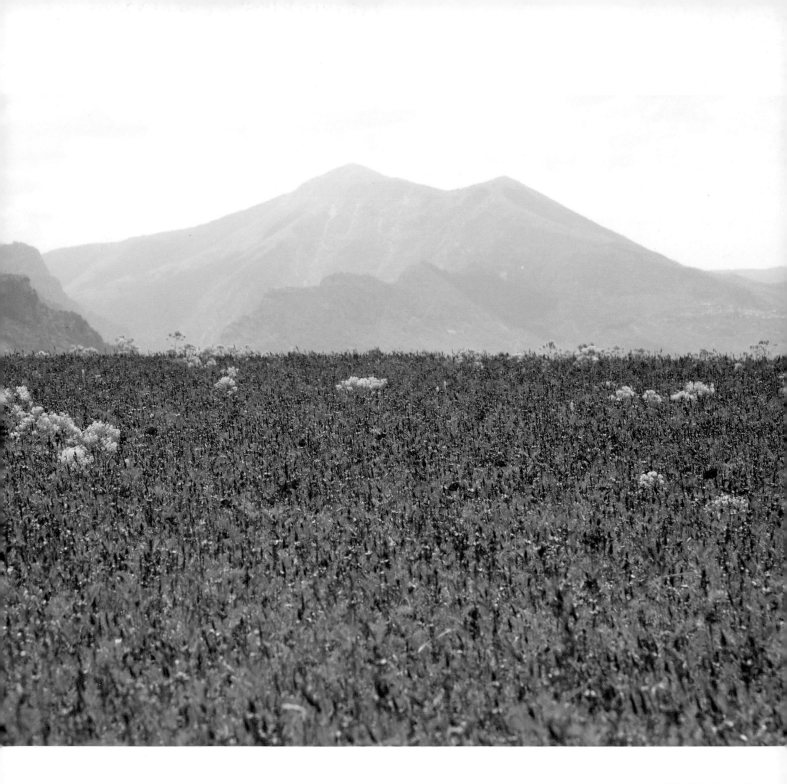

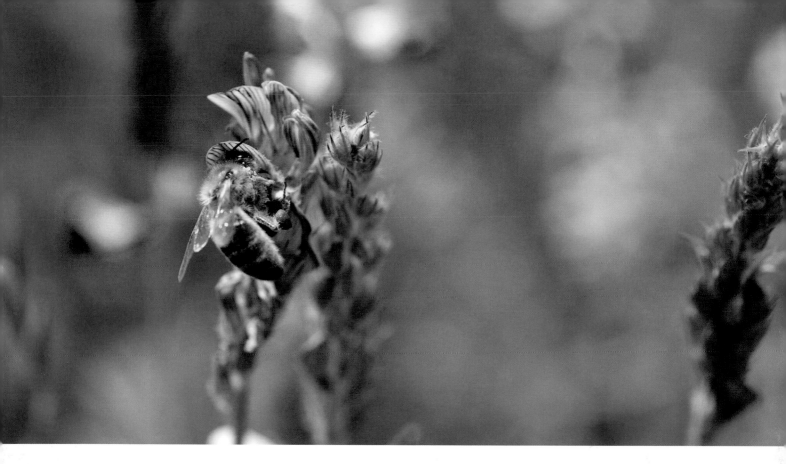

Tireless bees feast on a palette of flowers with exceptional aromas.

The seductive, candid, and uncomplicated flavors of Haute Provence's cuisine speak of the land, its geography, and its traditions. This is mountain country, and the food is simple, hearty, and unpretentious. The lean-yet-tender lamb of Sisteron is considered by food lovers to be among the best in France. It can be simply roasted with thyme, which grows wild everywhere, or prepared with artichokes and garlic. Herbs are used judiciously to flavor the food without overpowering, and everything is about balance.

Daube, a slow-cooked beef stew, is a staple; wild boar often finds its way into dishes, both on restaurant menus and in home cooking. *Pieds et paquets*, a robust dish of sheep's feet and stuffed tripe, is true mountain food. It's not for the faint of heart, but it's nonetheless worth trying with a robust red wine from the area. Chicken may be roasted with a delicate blend of herbs and sweetened with a touch of lavender honey.

Honey

As with wine and olive oil, the concept of *terroir* is important for honey. The honeys of Provence are the product of a very felicitous marriage between the impressive social structure of the bee hive and the incredible variety of flowers found in Provence.

Humans have included honey in their diet since ancient times. The civilizations of ancient Egypt, Greece, and Rome, as well as countless others, used honey to sweeten not just desserts, but also savory and spicy dishes. Today, the use of honey in cooking is less common, but many Provençal recipes include honey—to the joy of taste buds everywhere.

Truffles

A mysterious mushroom shrouded in legend, the black truffle (*Tuber melanosporum*; *rabasse* or *rabasso negro* in Provençal) thrives in the hills of Haute Provence, amidst its limestone soils and on truffle oaks. They are often called Périgord truffles after a region in southwestern France, but Provence is actually the main producer of black truffles. They are undeniably the most aromatic and flavorful of the 32 varieties of European truffles.

In the hills of Provence, the *rabasse* dominates, quickly taking over whatever tree it has chosen as its home. In the spring, its spores and seeds gather around the roots of oak and hazel trees, slowly forming a concentric zone in which little else survives. The *rabasse* grows there for a year, in the shade of its loving tree, attached to the roots, before it is harvested.

Winter is truffle season, and truffle hunters comb the hills daily, often accompanied by a well-trained pig or dog that can sniff out the black treasures. The truffles are sold at the markets in Aips, Apt, or Carpentras, attracting both professional chefs and amateur gourmets who hope to get their hands on some of these delicious treasures.

To make the most delectable truffle tartines (*crostinis de truffe*), grill slices of crusty bread and shave black truffle over them. A drizzle of olive oil and a pinch of *fleur de sel* or coarse Camargue sea salt complete a most delectable *apéritif!*

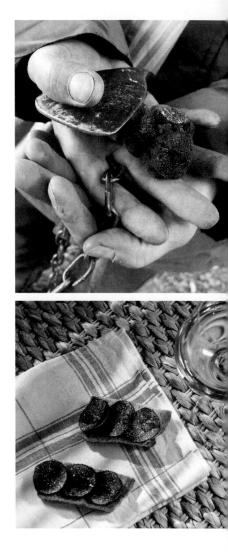

The black truffle has its own history and tales. It is the stuff of pleasure and dreams!

Chèvre

Chèvre, the famous French goat cheese, has a long history. More than 30 centuries ago, the people of the Mediterranean domesticated goats and started making cheese from their milk. Today, chèvre finds its way onto Provençal tables in many different forms, from young, soft, and creamy to firm, aged, and pungent. Of course, chèvre has a natural affinity with rosé: the two are a perfect combination and together evoke the spirit of Provence.

Chèvre is, of course, perfect with crusty bread, either simple *pain de campagne* or breads flavored with olives, herbs, and even figs. To preserve young chèvre, place it in a glass jar with some thyme, bay leaf, rosemary, and black peppercorns and cover with extra virgin olive oil. Refrigerate and serve at your leisure on toasted bread, accompanied by a glass of rosé ... *mais bien sûr!* Another option is to place several leaves of savory on fresh chèvre for a day or two and enjoy the extraordinary flavor it imparts. For a sweeter taste, pair young chèvre with fig *confiture* (jam) or Provençal honey. Dessert is served!

The goats from whose milk chèvre is made graze on the Mediterranean herbs of Provence. The herbs give their milk incredible flavor and aroma. Young chèvre, available from spring to fall, is soft and mild. Aged chèvre, available year round, is stronger in flavor and has a firm texture.

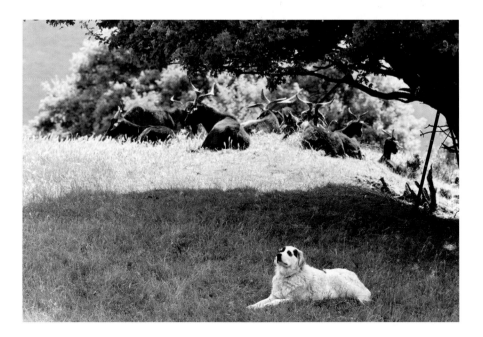

THE 13 DESSERTS

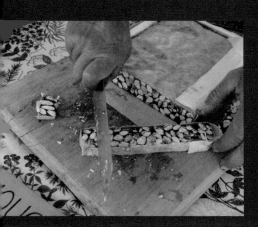

In early December, Provençals start gathering the makings of a centuries-old holiday tradition: the 13 desserts of Christmas Eve, which are served after *le gros souper* ("the big supper"). They represent Jesus and his 12 apostles, so tradition dictates that there must be 13 sweets and that each guest must have at least one bite of each.

The tradition of multiple desserts was first noted in historical documents in 1693, but the practice was formally established in the nineteenth and early twentieth centuries; the number 13 was fixed in 1920. *Pompe à l'huile* (brioche scented with orange blossom), nougat (white, red, or dark), dates, figs, prunes, dried apricots, walnuts, raisins, oranges, apples, pears, grapes, and other delicious treats have been part of this holiday tradition for centuries.

Over time, the fruits and sweets have changed, and each family has its own unique selection. But all over Provence, the ritual of a Christmas Eve big supper with family and friends always ends with 13 sweet bites.

Calissons

Calissons, a specialty of Aix-en-Provence, are marzipan-like confections with a base of ground sweet almonds and candied fruits (mostly melons and oranges) topped with royal icing. The almond-shaped candies come in all sizes and colors and adorn store windows all around Aix, tempting the taste buds.

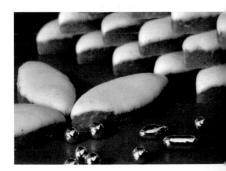

Some say *calissons* first appeared in 1473, in honor of the second marriage of King René. It's more likely they appeared much later, in the sixteenth century, when the first almonds arrived in Provence. Over time, Aix gradually became the center of the almond trade.

Aix is still home to numerous *calisson* makers, both big and small, and no visit to the elegant city is complete without enjoying a few *calissons*.

ANCHOÏADE WITH FRESH VEGETABLES

YIELD: 16–20 SERVINGS

4½–5 ounces (130 g) salt-packed anchovies (about 1 cup)

2 cloves garlic

6 tablespoons (90 mL) extra virgin olive oil

¼ teaspoon high-quality aged balsamic vinegar (optional)

2 cups (244 g) peeled and sliced carrots, for serving

2 cups (258 g) cherry or grape tomatoes, for serving

1 red pepper, cored and sliced, for serving

1 yellow pepper, cored and sliced, for serving

1 green pepper, cored and sliced, for serving

½ head cauliflower, cut into bite-sized pieces, for serving

1 seedless cucumber, sliced, for serving

2 ribs celery, cut into 2-inch (5-cm) pieces and sliced, for serving

1 Belgian endive, leaves separated, for serving

*A*nchoïade, a thick paste of anchovies, garlic, and oil, is one of the most typical Provençal foods. Because the quality of *anchoïade* depends on the quality of the ingredients, make sure to use high-quality, salt-packed anchovies. Traditional *anchoïade* does not contain vinegar, but you can brighten the flavor of your concoction by using a couple of drops of high-quality aged balsamic vinegar.

Anchoïade can be served on slices of toasted bread or as a dip for fresh seasonal vegetables. In the latter case, the dish changes every time depending on what vegetables are in season and abundant. So choose the best vegetables and have fun composing a new dish every time. Enjoy with friends and a glass of crisp rosé.

1. In a small mixing bowl, soak the anchovies in cold water for 15 minutes to get rid of any excess salt.

2. In the bowl of a food processor or blender, combine the anchovies, garlic, oil, and balsamic vinegar, if using. Blend to obtain a thick paste.

3. Transfer the *anchoïade* to a small serving bowl and serve surrounded by the raw vegetables and endive leaves.

COOKS' NOTE: *This delicious dish can also be accompanied by a tapenade, eggplant caviar, or simply* fleur de sel *and* fruité verte *olive oil.*

TAPENADE

— YIELD: 10–16 SERVINGS —

1 cup (134 g) pitted black olives

2 small tomatoes, chopped, seeds removed (about ½ cup [80 g])

2 cloves garlic

2 tablespoons extra virgin olive oil

1 tablespoon lemon juice

1 salt-cured anchovy, rinsed (optional, but highly recommended)

Tapenade is the quintessential Provençal dish. Usually served on toasted bread, it can also give flavor to roasted white fish. Traditionally, tapenade contains olives and capers; this "rebel" version is slightly lighter and zestier because of the tomatoes. Enjoy with a crisp rosé and plenty of good friends.

1. In the bowl of a food processor, combine all the ingredients and process to a chunky, thick paste.

2. Serve slathered on toasted bread.

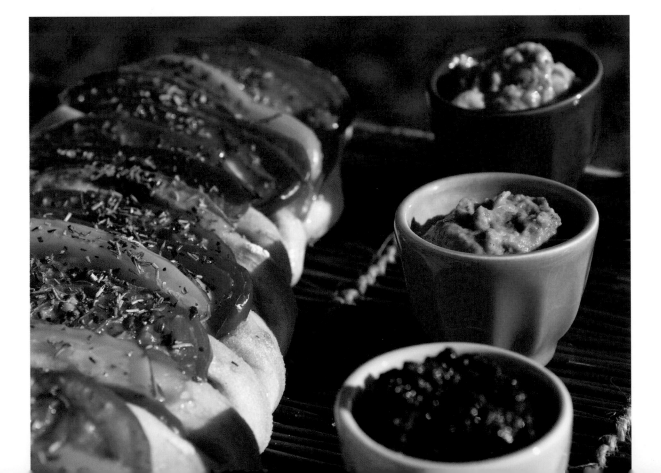

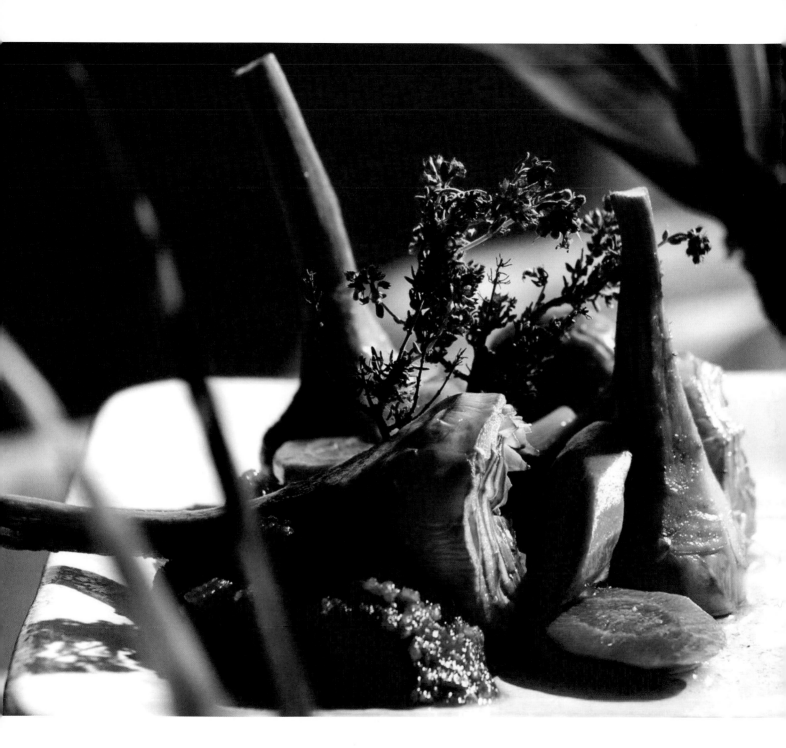

ARTICHOKES BARIGOULE

Artichauts en Barigoule

Juice of 1 lemon

8 fresh artichokes

2 tablespoons extra virgin olive oil

2 ounces (57 g) cubed bacon
or pancetta (about ⅓ cup)

1 medium onion, chopped
(about 1 cup [96 g])

2 large carrots, peeled and sliced

2 cloves garlic, minced

1 fresh bay leaf

1 tablespoon chopped fresh parsley

1 teaspoon minced fresh thyme

1 teaspoon sea salt, plus more to taste

1 cup (237 mL) dry white wine

Freshly ground black pepper, to taste

This typical Provençal recipe has changed a great deal over time and today, it barely resembles the original. *Barigoules*, which are a type of Provençal mushrooms, were the foundation of this recipe, but nowadays they are difficult to find. Over time, each Provençal developed his or her own variation on the dish. This version is rich, flavorful, and complex. It pairs well with both fuller-bodied whites and rosés.

1. Fill a medium bowl with water and add the lemon juice.

2. To clean the artichokes, start by cutting off the top third of each artichoke, including the thorny points. Remove the outer leaves by peeling them back until they snap. Using a paring knife, peel the stem to remove the fibrous outer layer. Remove any remaining tough, fibrous, dark green parts on the outside of the artichoke heart. With a spoon, scoop out the chokes and clean the inside of the artichoke. Immediately put the trimmed artichokes in the bowl of lemon water.

3. In a medium sauté pan warm the oil and bacon over medium-high heat. When the fat the starts to render, add the onion and cook for 5 to 6 minutes, until it starts to soften. Add the carrots and cook for 3 to 4 minutes. Add the garlic and cook for 1 minute.

4. Drain the artichokes, shaking off any excess water, and add them to the pan. Add the bay leaf, parsley, thyme, and 1 teaspoon of the salt. Stir well.

5. Add the wine and cook for 2 to 3 minutes, until the alcohol evaporates. Reduce the heat to low, cover, and cook for 40 to 45 minutes, until the artichokes can easily be pierced (add a little water during the cooking process if they become dried out). Remove from the heat.

6. Discard the bay leaf. Adjust the seasoning to taste and add a grind of the black pepper. Transfer to a serving dish. Serve warm.

LAYERED OMELETTES

Crespeou de Provence

20 large eggs

2 tablespoons chopped fresh basil

2 tablespoons chopped fresh parsley

2 teaspoon chopped fresh thyme

1 teaspoon sea salt, plus more to taste

Freshly ground black pepper, to taste

6 tablespoons (90 mL) extra virgin olive oil, divided

1 medium zucchini, cubed (about ¾ cup [90 g])

3 spring onions, chopped (about ½ cup [48 g])

1 large tomato, seeded and chopped (about 1 cup [96 g])

2 medium portabello mushrooms, chopped (about 1 cup [114 g])

1 red pepper, chopped

2 cups (120 g) fresh spinach

1 medium tomato, seeded and chopped, for garnish

This fascinating, traditional Provençal dish needs to be tasted to be understood. The flavors of the different omelettes work together perfectly, producing a whole that is much more than the sum of its parts. The fact that the dish can be prepared ahead of time makes it the perfect party dish. Pair with a lively Provence rosé and the party can begin.

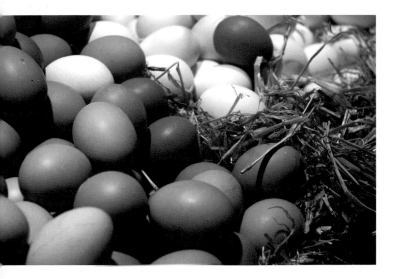

1. In a large mixing bowl, lightly beat the eggs and add the basil, parsley, thyme, salt, and a grind of the black pepper.

2. Preheat the oven to 350°F (180°C).

3. Place a shallow, ovenproof dish the same size as the pan you will use for the omelettes next to the stove.

4. In a small nonstick pan, warm 1 tablespoon of the oil over medium-high heat. Add the zucchini and cook for 5 to 7 minutes, until it softens. Add ⅙ of the egg mixture and make a soft omelette. Place the omelette in the prepared bowl.

5. In the same pan, warm another tablespoon of the oil. Add the spring onions and cook for 3 to 4 minutes, until they start to soften. Add ⅙ of the egg mixture and make a soft omelette. Transfer the omelette to the prepared bowl.

6. Warm another tablespoon of oil in the pan. Add the tomato and cook for 3 to 4 minutes, until it has released its liquid. Add ⅙ of the egg mixture and make a soft omelette. Transfer the omelette to the prepared bowl.

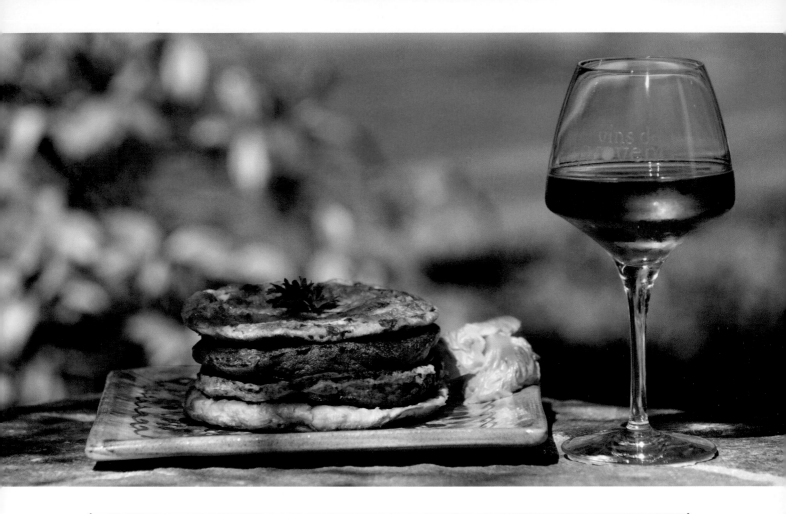

7. Warm another tablespoon of oil in the pan. Add the mushrooms and cook for 5 to 6 minutes, until they release their liquid. Add ⅙ of the egg mixture and make a soft omelette. Transfer the omelette to the prepared bowl.

8. Warm another tablespoon of oil in the pan. Add the pepper and cook for 3 to 4 minutes. Add ⅙ of the egg mixture and make a soft omelette. Transfer the omelette to the prepared bowl.

9. Warm the remaining tablespoon of oil in the pan. Add the remaining egg mixture and spinach and make a soft omelette. Remove from the heat. Transfer the omelette to the prepared bowl.

10. Bake for 35 to 40 minutes. Remove from the oven and set aside to cool to room temperature. Transfer the layered omelettes to the refrigerator for several hours or overnight.

11. Invert the layered omelettes onto a serving platter and slice. Serve cold, garnished with chopped tomato.

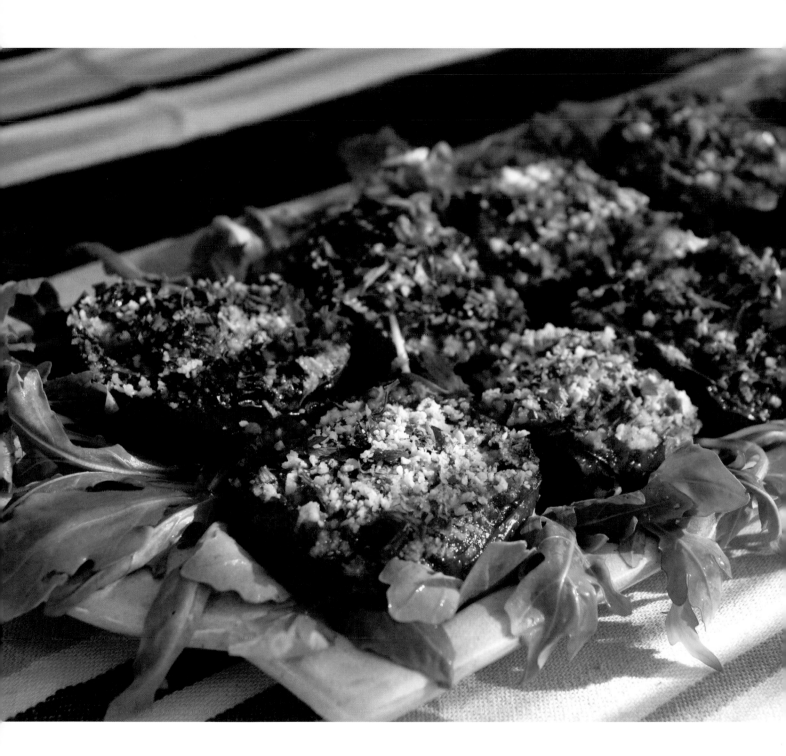

TOMATOES PROVENÇAL

Tomates à la Provençale

— YIELD: 4 SERVINGS —

4 small to medium ripe tomatoes, halved and stems removed

1 teaspoon granulated sugar

2 tablespoons extra virgin olive oil

½ cup (64 g) chopped fresh parsley

4 cloves garlic, minced

2 tablespoons fresh breadcrumbs

½ teaspoon sea salt, plus more to taste

Freshly ground black pepper, to taste

This traditional Provençal dish relies on the quality of the tomatoes used; they must be fresh and ripe. It's best to prepare this dish in the summer, when tomatoes are at the peak of ripeness, sweet, and full of flavor. The traditional preparation is on the stovetop, as in this recipe. It can also be made in the oven, but the tomatoes caramelize better on the stovetop. Serve as a light meal with other Provençal delicacies and some crusty bread, or with meat.

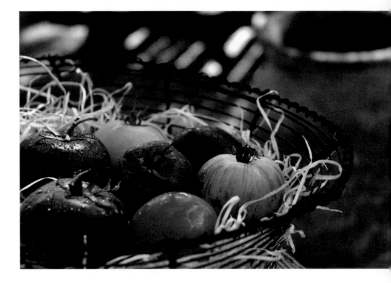

1. Lightly dust the cut sides of the tomatoes with the sugar.

2. In a large sauté pan, warm the oil over medium heat. Add the tomatoes, cut sides down, and cook for 5 to 6 minutes, until they caramelize.

3. In a small mixing bowl, combine the parsley and garlic.

4. Flip the tomatoes and distribute the parsley and garlic mixture evenly onto them, pressing down so the mixture adheres to the tomato. Sprinkle with the ½ teaspoon of salt and the black pepper. Distribute the breadcrumbs evenly among the tomatoes.

5. Reduce the heat to low, cover, and cook for 5 to 6 minutes, until the tomatoes are soft and fully cooked through. Remove from the heat. Adjust the seasoning to taste.

6. Transfer the tomatoes to a serving dish and serve warm.

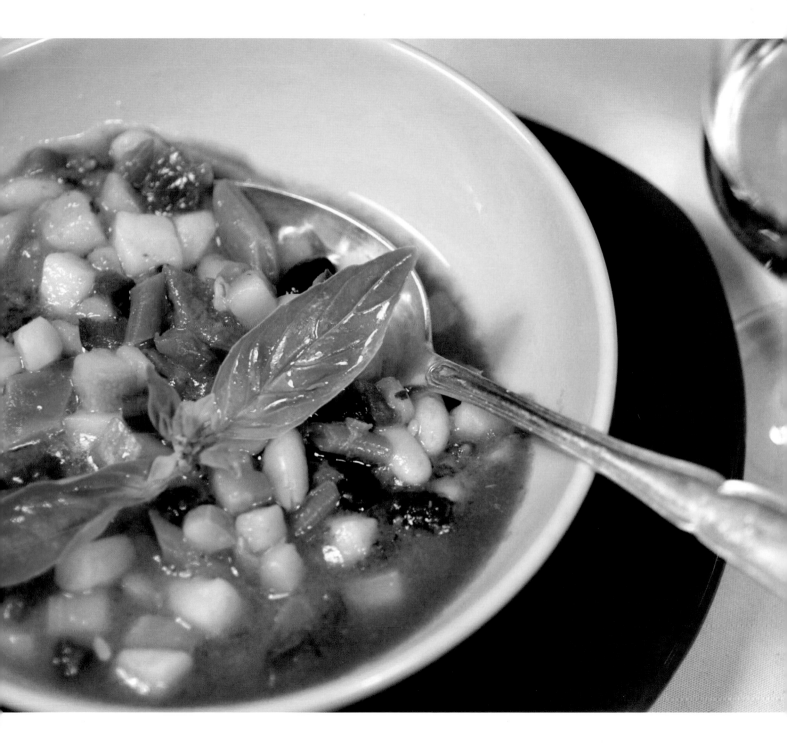

VEGETABLE SOUP WITH *PISTOU*

Soupe au Pistou

FOR THE SOUP:

4 quarts (3.80 L) water

½ pound (227 g) fresh shelled cannellini beans (about 1½ cups)

½ pound (227 g) fresh shelled borlotti (cranberry) beans (about 1½ cups)

2 fresh bay leaves

1 teaspoon minced fresh thyme

1½ teaspoons sea salt, divided, plus more to taste

½ teaspoon minced fresh rosemary

½ pound (227 g) haricots verts, cut into bite-sized pieces

½ pound (227 g) snow peas, cut into bite-sized pieces

4 medium potatoes, cubed

4 medium zucchini, cubed

1 medium onion, chopped

2 small tomatoes, seeded and chopped

Freshly ground black pepper, to taste

FOR THE *PISTOU*:

1 tomato, peeled, seeded, and chopped

3 garlic cloves

1 cup fresh basil

⅓ cup (79 mL) extra virgin olive oil

2 tablespoons grated Parmigiano–Reggiano cheese

½ teaspoon sea salt

This soup speaks of Provence: sun, fresh breezes, and summer vegetables full of flavor. The most important thing is to use seasonally available vegetables, including fresh beans. So, at the height of summer, take a trip to the farmers' market, choose the best produce, and enjoy a bowl of Provence wherever you are. The soup can be served hot or cold, with the *pistou* added at the last minute and, of course, a glass of chilled, fresh Provence rosé.

TO PREPARE THE SOUP:

1. Place the water in a medium stockpot over medium-high heat. Add the cannellini and borlotti beans, bay leaves, thyme, 1 teaspoon of the salt, and the rosemary. Bring to a boil, lower the heat to medium-low, and cook for 30 minutes.

2. Add the haricots verts, snow peas, and potatoes and cook for another 10 minutes.

3. Add the zucchini, onion, tomatoes, and the remaining ½ teaspoon of the salt and cook for 20 minutes. Remove from the heat. Remove and discard the bay leaves and season to taste with the salt and black pepper.

TO PREPARE THE *PISTOU*:

1. As the soup cooks, combine all the *pistou* ingredients in the bowl of a food processor or blender. Pulse to obtain a thick sauce. Transfer the *pistou* to a small bowl.

TO ASSEMBLE THE DISH:

1. Transfer the soup to a serving dish and serve immediately as a hot dish, or chill in the refrigerator and serve cold. Pass the *pistou* on the side for guests to add as desired.

WILD BOAR STEW

Daube de Sanglier

FOR THE *BOUQUET GARNI*:

5 whole black peppercorns

4 whole cloves

4 sprigs fresh thyme

2 fresh bay leaves

2 sprigs fresh rosemary

2 sprigs fresh sage

FOR MARINATING THE BOAR:

1 bottle full-bodied red wine

3 medium carrots, sliced

1 large yellow onion, thinly sliced

3 cloves garlic

4 pounds (1.82 kg) wild boar shoulder, cubed

FOR THE STEW:

¼ cup (59 mL) extra virgin olive oil, plus more for drizzling

5–6 slices pancetta, cubed (about ½ cup [75–85 g])

3 tablespoons (23 g) flour

½ cup (72 g) Kalamata olives, chopped

1 teaspoon sea salt, plus more to taste

Freshly ground black pepper, to taste

2 cups (228 g) fresh mushrooms, chopped or 1 cup (56 g) dried mushrooms

Wild boars roam the mountains of Provence. A delicacy, boar meat is cooked for a long time over a low fire. It pairs well with robust reds from the AOC Coteaux d'Aix en Provence or AOC Côtes de Provence Sainte-Victoire. Serve this dish with Creamy Polenta (see recipe on p. 78) and Fried Chanterelles (see recipe on p. 78) for a feast you won't soon forget.

TO PREPARE THE *BOUQUET GARNI*:

1. In a small piece of cheesecloth, combine all the ingredients for the *bouquet garni*. Tie the cheesecloth closed with a piece of kitchen twine, like a sachet. Set aside.

TO MARINATE THE BOAR:

1. In a large mixing bowl, combine the ingredients for the marinade. Add the *bouquet garni* and the boar.

2. Cover and place in the refrigerator for 12 hours to overnight.

TO PREPARE THE STEW:

1. Remove the boar from the refrigerator. Remove from the marinade and pat dry with paper towels. Reserve the bowl of marinade. Discard the *bouquet garni*.

2. In a large stockpot, warm the oil over medium-high heat. Add the pancetta and cook for 3 to 4 minutes, until the fat renders. Add the onions, carrots, and garlic from the reserved marinade and cook for 8 to 10 minutes, until the vegetables start to soften. Add the boar and flour, stir well, and cook for 5 to 7 minutes.

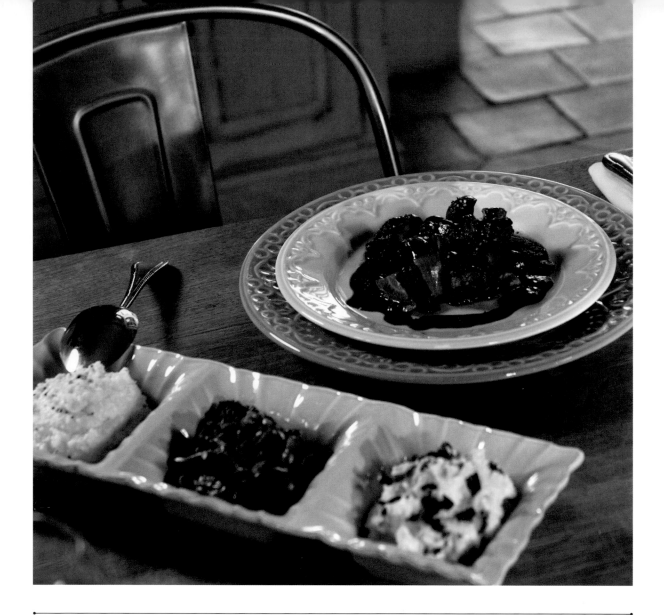

3.   Add the rest of the reserved marinade, 1 teaspoon of the salt, and a grind of the black pepper and bring to a boil. Reduce the heat to low, cover, and cook for 3 hours, stirring occasionally. Add the olives and mushrooms and continue cooking for another 30 minutes. Remove from the heat.

4.   Transfer the stew to a serving dish. Finish with a drizzle of the oil. Serve hot.

COOKS' NOTE: *When the stew is done, add 2 squares of dark chocolate (at least 80%) and stir well. This will give the stew a shine and add depth to its flavor.*

CREAMY POLENTA

Polenta Crémeuse

YIELD: 4 SERVINGS

7 cups (1.66 L) 2% or whole milk
1 cup (237 mL) half-and-half
2 cups (140 g) coarse polenta
1 ½ teaspoons sea salt, plus more to taste
2 tablespoons unsalted butter
Freshly ground black pepper, to taste

1. In a medium saucepan, warm the milk and half-and-half over medium heat. Slowly add the polenta, stirring constantly to break up any lumps. Add the salt, reduce the heat to low, and continue cooking for at least 40 minutes (up to 1 hour). Remove from the heat.

2. Add the butter and season to taste with salt and black pepper. Stir well, transfer to a serving bowl, and serve immediately.

FRIED CHANTERELLES

Chanterelles Poêlées

YIELD: 4 SERVINGS

2 tablespoons unsalted butter
½ pound (227 g) chanterelle mushrooms, cleaned
Sea salt and freshly ground black pepper, to taste
1 teaspoon minced fresh chives

Chanterelle mushrooms are at their most delicious when prepared simply. The rich, earthy flavor adds complexity to creamy polenta or pasta. They are also great on toasted bread as an appetizer. Pair with a robust-yet-elegant red from Coteaux d'Aix-en-Provence.

1. In a medium sauté pan, melt the butter over medium-high heat. Add the chanterelles and cook for 4 to 5 minutes. Remove from the heat and season to taste with the salt and black pepper.

2. Transfer to a serving dish and sprinkle with the chives. Serve hot.

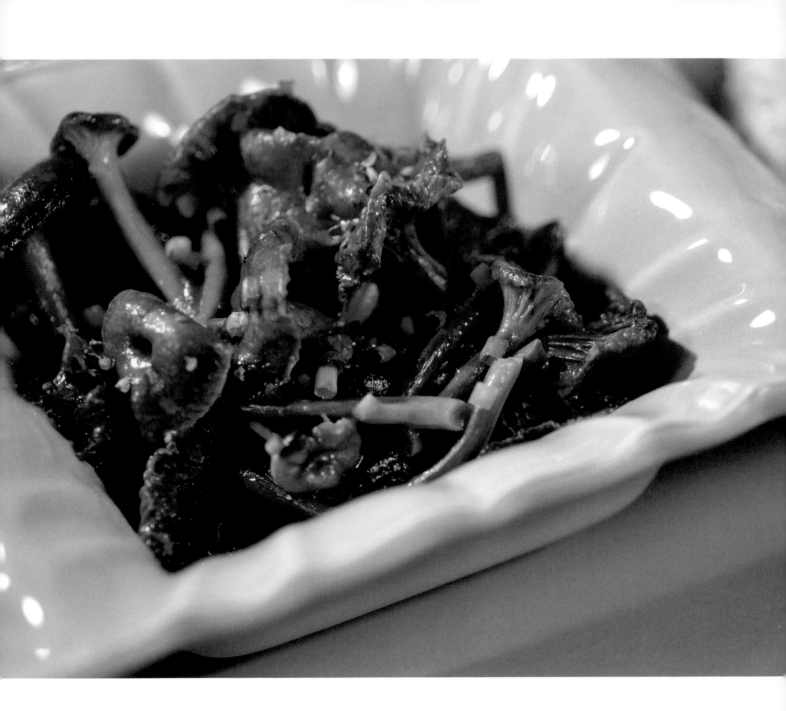

LANGOUSTINES WITH WATERCRESS, PANCETTA CREAM, AND ASPARAGUS

Langoustines avec des Cressons, Velouté de Jambon de Montagne, et des Asperges

—— YIELD: 4 SERVINGS ——

FOR THE LIME-GINGER SAUCE:

Juice of 3 limes

1 ounce (28 g) grated fresh ginger

1 clove garlic, minced

1 tablespoon soy sauce

FOR THE *BOUQUET GARNI*:

4 fresh sage leaves

2 sprigs fresh thyme

1 sprig fresh rosemary

FOR THE PANCETTA CREAM:

3 tablespoons (45 mL) extra virgin olive oil

2 medium onions, chopped

2 cloves garlic

½ pound (227 g) pancetta (or bacon), diced

½ cup (119 mL) fish (or vegetable) stock

⅓ cup (79 mL) half-and-half

Pinch ground *piment d'Espelette,* unsmoked hot paprika, cayenne, pimento, or Aleppo pepper

Sea salt and freshly ground black pepper, to taste

FOR ASSEMBLING THE DISH:

1 tablespoon extra virgin olive oil

2 cups (68 g) watercress

4 quail eggs, poached

4 stalks young asparagus, diced

4 pearl onions, blanched in salted water and halved

8 langoustines, steamed

Chef Xavier Mathieu of Le Phébus & Spa, a Relais & Châteaux hotel in Gordes Joucas, reimagines traditional Provençal dishes with a modern sensitivity and creative flair. This recipe is adjusted for home use, but the original dish is worth a trip to Chef Mathieu's dining room. Pair this delicious and sophisticated dish with a well-structured dry rosé from Coteaux d'Aix-en-Provence.

TO PREPARE THE LIME-GINGER SAUCE:

1. In a small mixing bowl, combine all the ingredients and set aside for at least 2 hours.

TO PREPARE THE *BOUQUET GARNI:*

1. In a little sachet, combine all the ingredients for the *bouquet garni.* Tie up the sachet to enclose the ingredients.

TO PREPARE THE PANCETTA CREAM:

1. In a medium sauté pan, warm the oil over medium heat. Add the onions and cook for 7 to 8 minutes, until they soften. Add the garlic and cook for another minute. Add the *bouquet garni* and pancetta and continue cooking for 3 to 4 minutes, until the fat has rendered. Add the stock and cook for 3 to 4 minutes. Remove from the heat.

2. Add the half-and-half and *piment d'Espelette* and stir well. Set aside for 10 minutes.

3. Strain the cream sauce through a chinois or other fine-mesh sieve. Discard the contents of the sieve. Season to taste with the salt and black pepper.

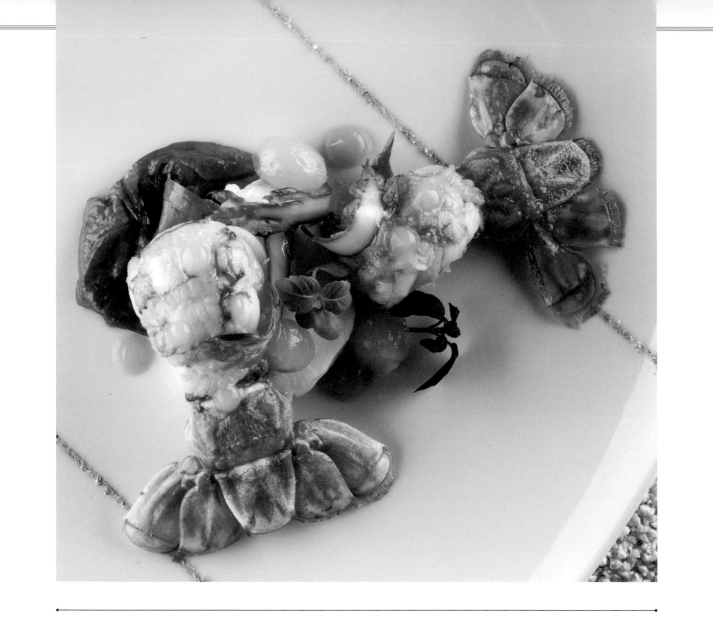

TO ASSEMBLE THE DISH:

1.   In a medium sauté pan, warm the oil over medium heat. Add the watercress and cook for 1 minute, until just wilted. Remove from the heat.

2.   Distribute the watercress among 4 plates. Add 1 poached egg, some asparagus, and 2 pearl onion halves to each plate. Add 2 langoustine tails to each plate. Drizzle some lime–ginger sauce around the langoustines. Serve the pancetta cream on the side.

COOKS' NOTE: *You can substitute poached chicken eggs for the quail eggs.*

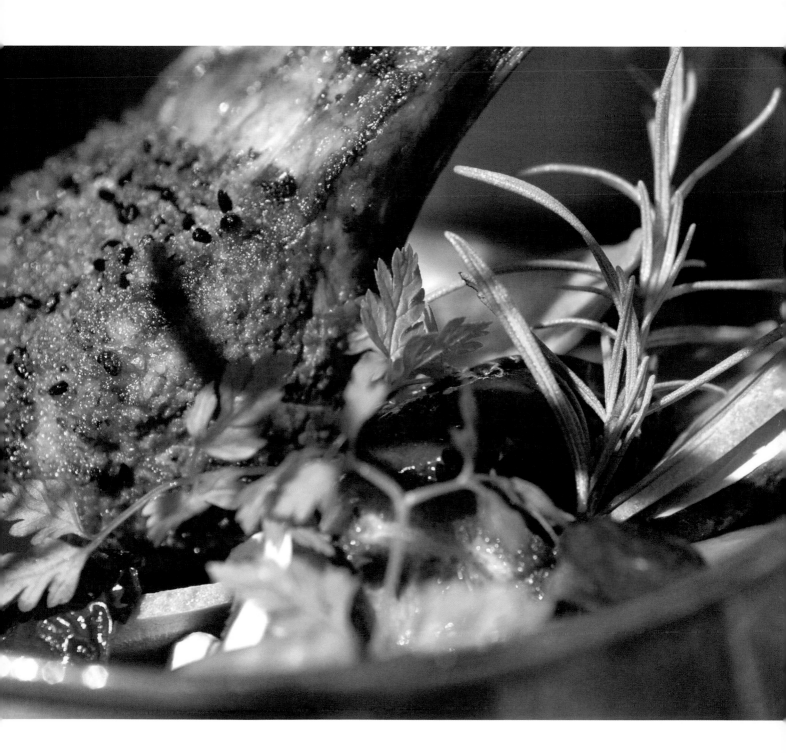

RACK OF LAMB WITH VEGETABLES

Carré d'Agneau Pané aux Légumes Croquants et aux Cèpes

FOR THE LAMB:

2 tablespoons extra virgin olive oil

½ teaspoon cumin

½ teaspoon sea salt

I 2-pound (908 g) rack of lamb

½ cup (50 g) fresh breadcrumbs

FOR THE VEGETABLES:

¼ cup (40 g) cubed pancetta

3 carrots, peeled and sliced

¾ pound (341 g) haricots verts

I spring onion, chopped

½ teaspoon chopped fresh thyme

½ teaspoon chopped fresh rosemary

½ cup (57 g) sliced fresh mushrooms

Sea salt, to taste

Provençal lamb has aromas of *garrigue*, the bushes, plants, and aromatic herbs covering the dry hills of Provence. It makes the lamb extremely succulent and best when prepared simply, with some quickly cooked, still-crunchy vegetables.

The wine should be supple with a note of forest floor and mushroom. A full-bodied red from the interior of Provence is the perfect pairing for this dish that's both elegant and hearty.

TO PREPARE THE LAMB:

1. Preheat the oven to 375°F (190°C).

2. In a small mixing bowl, combine the oil, cumin, and salt. Rub the rack of lamb with the mixture, then sprinkle with the breadcrumbs. Roast the lamb in a pan for 10 to 15 minutes, until the lamb reaches an internal temperature of 130°F. Remove from the oven and let rest for 10 minutes.

TO PREPARE THE VEGETABLES:

1. In a large sauté pan, warm the pancetta over medium heat. When the fat has rendered, add the carrots and cook for 2 to 3 minutes. Add the haricots verts, onion, and herbs, stir well, and cook for another 4 minutes. Remove from the heat, add the mushrooms, and set aside.

2. Transfer the lamb and the vegetables to the same serving dish. Season with salt to taste. Serve warm, drizzled with the cooking juices.

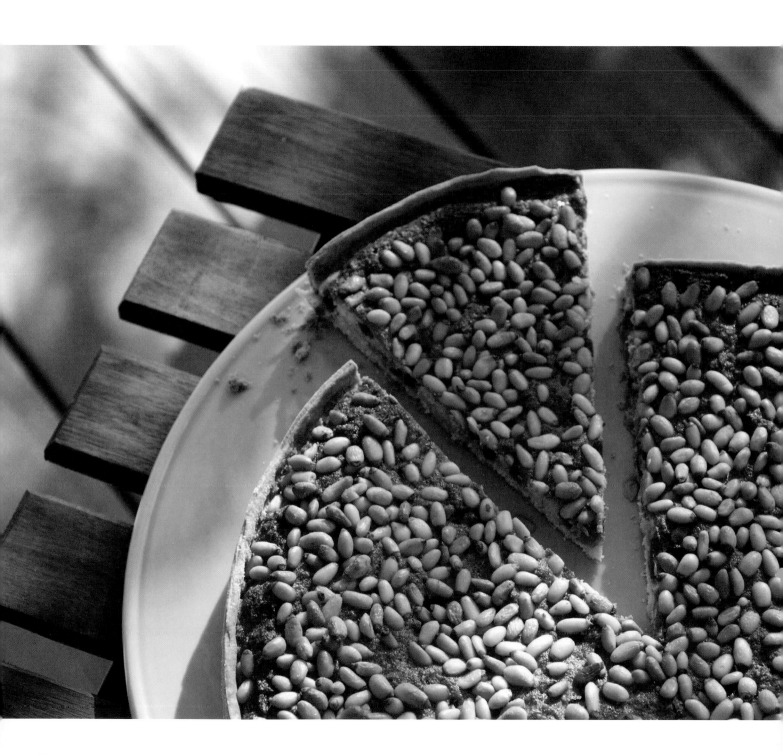

PINE NUT TART

Tarte aux Pignons

FOR THE PASTRY SHELL:

1¼ cups (156 g) all-purpose flour

1 teaspoon granulated sugar

½ teaspoon sea salt

1 stick chilled butter, cubed (8 tablespoons)

¼ cup (59 mL) ice water

FOR THE FILLING:

2 tablespoons raisins

4 tablespoons (59 mL) rum, divided

½ cup (71 g) apricot or peach *confiture* (jam)

6 tablespoons (34 g) butter

5 tablespoons (60 g) granulated sugar

2 eggs

1 cup (170 g) ground almonds

½ cup (68 g) pine nuts, roughly chopped

This rich and delicious tart is perfect for an afternoon snack with tea or coffee, or as a dessert after a light dinner.

TO PREPARE THE PASTRY SHELL:

1. In the bowl of a food processor, combine the flour, sugar, and salt. Add the butter and pulse for 15 seconds, until the dough resembles coarse meal.

2. Slowly add the water, continuing to pulse for another 15 seconds, until clumps start to form. Do not overprocess. The dough should not be a solid ball.

3. Transfer the dough to an unfloured work surface and gently form into a ball. Divide into two, and flatten each half into a disc. Wrap the discs in plastic wrap and refrigerate at least 40 minutes. At this point, the dough can be frozen for up to 1 month.

4. Remove 1 disc of the dough from the refrigerator and set aside at room temperature until it starts to soften and can be rolled out. The dough should not be too soft, as it will stick.

5. Between 2 sheets of plastic wrap or wax paper, roll out the dough to a ¼-inch (6-mm) thickness.

6. Transfer the dough to a 9-inch (22.5-cm) tart pan with a removable bottom, and press into the bottom and the flutes of the tart pan. Trim off any excess dough.

TO PREPARE THE FILLING:

1. Preheat the oven to 375°F (190°C).

2. In a cup, soak the raisins in 2 tablespoons of the rum for at least 2 hours or overnight.

3. In a small mixing bowl, combine the *confiture* and the remaining 2 tablespoons of the rum.

4. In a medium mixing bowl, combine the butter and sugar. Beat with an electric mixer on low speed until creamy. Add the eggs and continue beating on medium speed until the eggs are incorporated. Add the ground almonds and beat for 1 minute, until the mixture is uniform. Add the *confiture* mixture and the raisin mixture and stir well.

5. Pour the filling into the prepared tart shell and distribute evenly.

6. Distribute the pine nuts evenly on the tart and bake for 35 minutes, until the crust and top are golden brown. Remove from the oven and serve at room temperature.

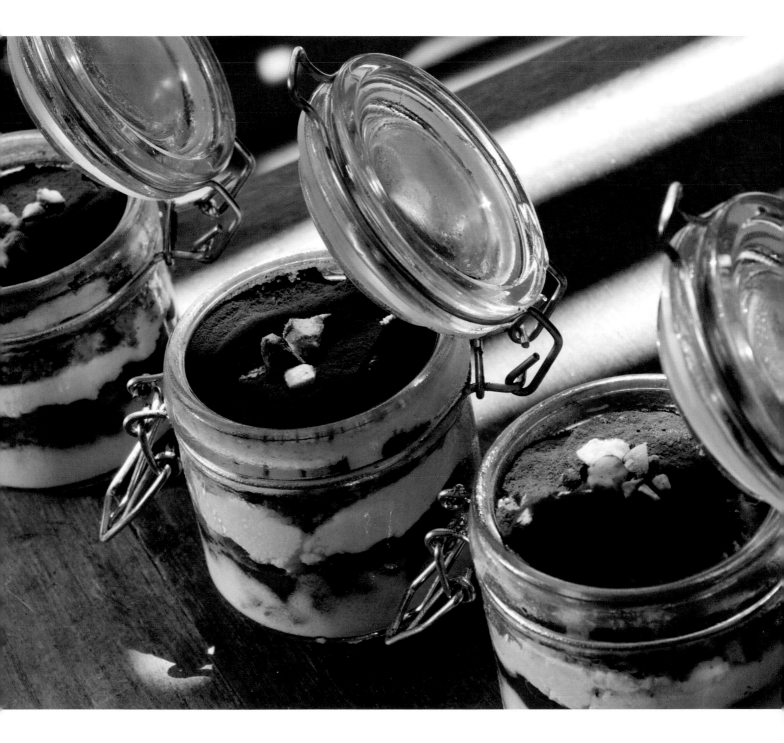

STRAWBERRY TIRAMISÙ

Tiramisù de Fraises Présenté en Bocaux

YIELD: 4 SERVINGS

FOR THE STRAWBERRY TARTAR:

1 cup (144 g) strawberries, sliced

1 tablespoon granulated sugar

Juice of ½ lime

FOR THE TIRAMISÙ:

3 eggs

½ cup (96 g) granulated sugar, divided

8 ounces (227 g) mascarpone cheese

½ cup (56 g) unsalted shelled pistachios, toasted and chopped

1 ½ tablespoons cocoa powder

This delicious summer dessert is the perfect ending to a Provençal party: feather-light and silky.

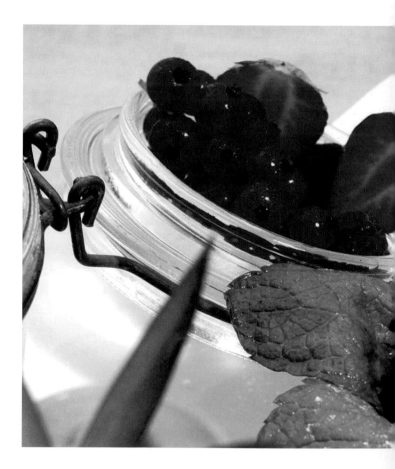

TO PREPARE THE STRAWBERRY TARTAR:

1. In a medium mixing bowl, combine the strawberries, sugar, and lime juice. Set aside.

TO PREPARE THE TIRAMISÙ:

1. Crack the eggs, separating the yolks into a small mixing bowl and the whites in a medium mixing bowl.

2. Add ¼ cup (48 g) of the sugar to the bowl of yolks. Beat until thick and white. Set aside.

3. Add the remaining ¼ cup (48 g) of the sugar to the bowl of whites. Beat to soft peaks.

4. Fold together the egg yolk and egg white mixtures. Add the mascarpone and fold together.

5. In each of 4 mason jars, place 1 tablespoon of the egg–mascarpone mixture, then some strawberry tartar, more egg–mascarpone mixture, and a layer of pistachios. Finish with a layer of the egg–mascarpone mixture. Refrigerate until ready to serve.

6. Before serving, remove the jars from the refrigerator and dust the surfaces with the cocoa powder. Serve chilled.

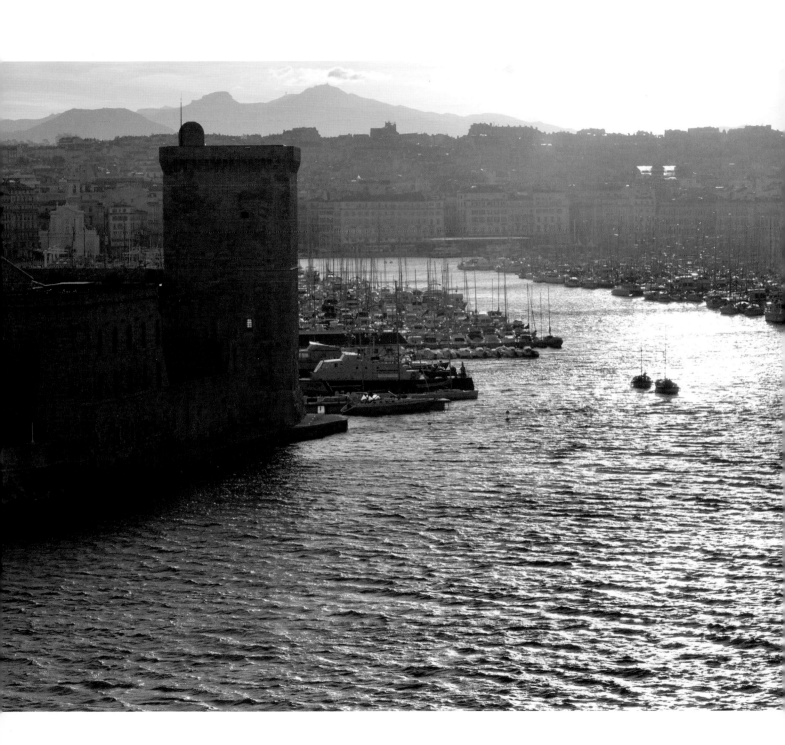

Marseille

MARSEILLE IS THE SECOND LARGEST CITY IN FRANCE AND ALSO one of the oldest cities in the country. Founded around 600 BCE by Greek sailors, the ensuing 26 centuries have created a multilayered city with rich culture and traditions, and a complex blend of influences. Marseille is a city with character—a true Mediterranean port.

Today, Marseille is a vibrant, modern, cosmopolitan city. But, in the past it has struggled with poverty, and the cooking reflects that. Based on fresh, local ingredients, it also represents the quintessential Mediterranean diet. Fresh fish caught locally is at the heart of the Marseille cooking. To this day, Vieux Port ("Old Port"), the main harbor, belongs to the locals who dutifully come to market to buy their fish and exchange news with the fishermen and women. Visitors and travelers might come to admire the fish and take pictures, but it is the locals, the people who have been buying their fish here for generations, who are the soul of the fish market.

Marseille is a large port, so it's easy to think of its food as being mostly sea based. But, as in the rest of Provence, flavorful vegetables also grow here and create the foundation of many dishes. The preparations are simple, but what gives the cooking of Marseille a unique touch are the many influences that its diverse population has brought from near and far, places such as Turkey, Lebanon, Sicily, Corsica, Tunisia, and Armenia. So, couscous, exotic spices,

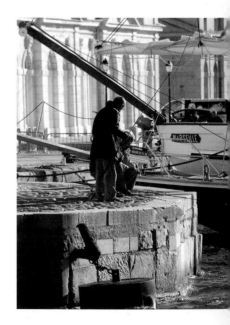

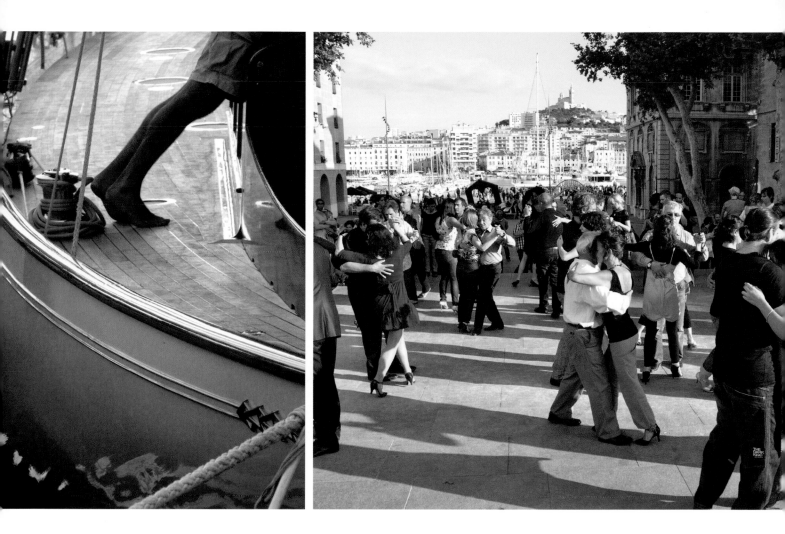

and Middle Eastern sweets drenched in syrup rub shoulders in the streets of Marseille with *bouillabaisse*, that iconic fish stew of the city, and *panisse*, the fried snack of chickpea flour that pairs so well with the local La Cagole beer. There is also a strong Italian influence, due to immigrants from Italy who brought pizza with them, which Marseille has adopted and continues to worship.

And then there are the unique sweets scented with orange blossom: *navettes*, the crunchy cookies that have become the symbol of Marseille, and *pompe*, a round brioche that makes the perfect mid-morning snack.

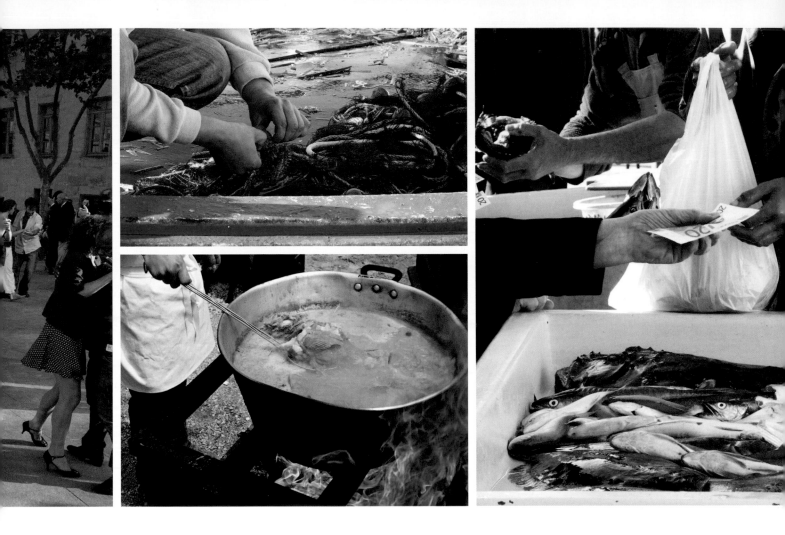

If you happen to be walking in the Vieux Port and see fishermen or boat owners grilling sardines, stop for a second and inhale deeply. And, if you are lucky and they offer you a sardine, take it; it will be the most memorable one you've ever had.

Like the city itself, its foods are a mélange and difficult to pin down, but deliciously seductive. Marseille celebrates this diversity unselfconsciously and proudly. Its vibrant culture and traditions are at the center of its modern and refined cuisine, a cuisine created by young and dynamic chefs, who are inspired by many influences yet remain true to tradition.

Marseille is a very cosmopolitan city. Here, all of the Mediterranean cultures intersect and descend upon the Vieux Port, which is always humming with activity.

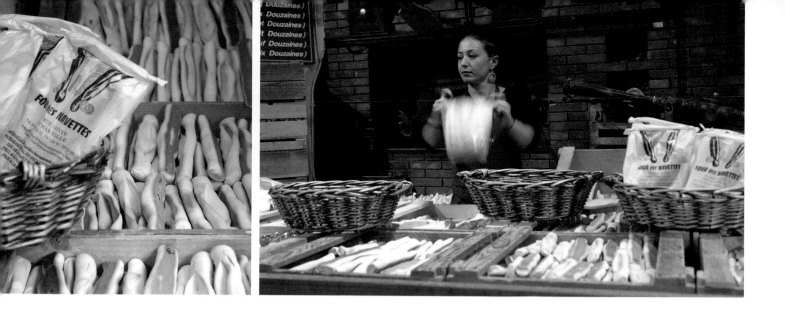

Navettes

Navettes, a specialty of Marseille, are long, delicate, boat-shaped cookies, traditionally scented with orange blossom. Some link the history of *navettes* to celebrations at the Abbey of Saint Victor in Marseille. The more romantic story is that the *navette* represents the boat that brought Mary Magdalene, Mary Salome, and Mary Jacobe (believed to be the first witnesses of the empty tomb at the resurrection of Jesus) to the coast of Provence after they were cast adrift while sailing from Alexandria, Egypt.

Less traditional varieties are flavored with a blend of spices and have a denser texture, more similar to *sablé*, the delicate French shortbread cookie. But the people of Marseille still swear by Four des Navettes, the oldest bakery in Marseille, which has remained a family business since it opened in 1781. For over 200 years, the bakery has zealously guarded the recipe for its most famous delicacy, and both locals and travelers alike dutifully make the trek up the steep hill and patiently stand in line to buy a couple dozen *navettes* to share with friends as they stroll through Vieux Port. The crunchy outside hides a light and feathery inside that melts in the mouth, caressing the taste buds with just a hint of sweetness and the tantalizing aromas of orange blossom.

So, as they say at Four des Navettes, "Come aboard, have a taste, and make the journey … it'll be one you never forget!"

GRILLED SARDINES

Sardines Grillées

— YIELD: 4 SERVINGS —

Extra virgin olive oil, for brushing

1 ½ pounds (681 g) fresh sardines (or sardine fillets), cleaned

Sea salt, to taste

1 lemon, for juicing

Grilled sardines are Marseille's specialty. Any self-respecting Provençal will tell you emphatically that in Nice, the sardines are stuffed, but in Marseille, they are simply grilled. Walking around Marseille's Vieux Port, you'll see fishermen and boat owners grilling sardines by the side of their boats, as they sip on rosé and exchange news with their neighbors, all under the benevolent gaze of *la bonne mère* (the nickname for the city's patron, a statue of Madonna that sits atop the Notre-Dame de la Garde). On our first visit to Marseille, we passed a large gathering of people sitting family style at long wood tables, while a woman quickly flipped dozens of sardines on a nearby grill, trying to keep up with the hungry crowd. The aroma was so seductive that we stopped to admire the scene. Next thing we knew, the woman was handing us grilled sardines through the chain link fence. With nothing but a little olive oil and a sprinkling of salt, the fish had the flavor of a real sardine, assertive without being aggressive. The charred skin protected the moist flesh, each bite a perfect combination of the two. It is a taste memory we have recreated in this recipe. In Marseille, your fingers are the only utensils you need for eating grilled sardines, so to capture the spirit of Marseille, try it!

This is the perfect grilling dish: simple and easy, so you can relax and chat with your friends while sipping a glass of chilled rosé. The best way to grill sardines is on a flat-top grill sprinkled with some coarse sea salt. If using a regular grill, turn the sardines very carefully with a spatula, as they are fragile and break easily.

1. Preheat the grill and brush with the oil. Season the sardines with the salt.

2. Add the sardines and grill for 2 minutes on each side, turning them carefully so as not to break them. Serve immediately with a drizzle of lemon juice.

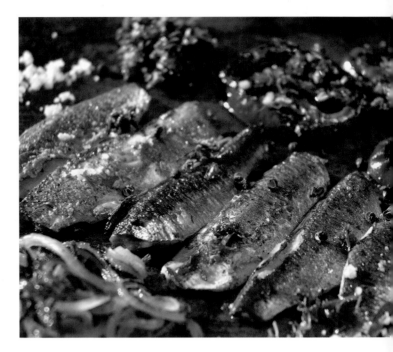

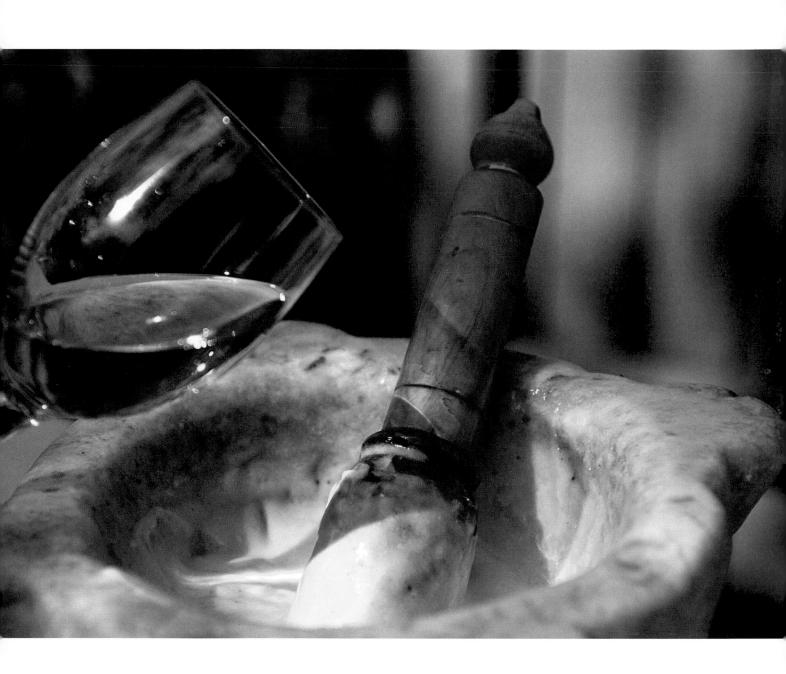

AÏOLI

FOR THE VEGETABLES AND COD:

3 cups (711 mL) vegetable stock

1 pound (454 g) salt cod, cut into 1-inch (2.5-cm) pieces and soaked in cold water for at least 24 hours

1½ cups (356 mL) water

1 pound (454 g) carrots, peeled and cut into 2-inch (5-cm) pieces

1 pound (454 g) haricots verts

6 hard-boiled eggs, quartered

FOR THE AÏOLI:

5 cloves garlic

1 teaspoon sea salt

3 small potatoes, boiled

1 cup (237 mL) mild Provençal extra virgin olive oil

This cornerstone of Provençal food was traditionally eaten on Ash Wednesday, as part of the big Christmas dinner, or on Fridays. But, of course, any day you have the urge to enjoy some aïoli, by all means do so.

Aïoli is usually the center of a large array of fresh and steamed vegetables, fish, and boiled potatoes. The garlic base gives aïoli its name (from ail, French for "garlic"). The garlic also makes aïoli linger on the palate, making it ill advised to kiss anyone who has not partaken of the dish.

Aïoli is the source of heated debate in Provence. For non-Provençals, aïoli may be just a variation of mayonnaise (Provençals call this "Parisian aïoli"), but true Provençals know better. Traditionally, as François's grandmother made it, the sauce started with garlic, salt, and three well-cooked potatoes (and, of course, a lot of exertion with the mortar and pestle). Olive oil is added slowly and, after much vigorous stirring, the sauce comes together. Yes, traditional aïoli requires effort, but it is worthwhile.

There's one point everyone can agree on: The best thing after a feast of aïoli is a siesta under a fig tree.

TO PREPARE THE VEGETABLES AND COD:

1. In a medium saucepan, bring the stock to a boil over medium-high heat. Reduce the heat to medium-low and add the cod. Cook for 4 to 5 minutes. With a slotted spoon, remove the cod and set aside on a plate lined with paper towels. Remove from the heat.

2. In a separate medium saucepan with a steaming basket insert, bring the water to a boil over high heat. Add the carrots and cook for 3 to 4 minutes, until they start to soften. Remove the carrots from the steaming basket and set aside.

3. Add the haricots verts to the steaming basket and cook for 2 to 3 minutes, until they start to soften. Remove from the heat. Remove from the basket and set aside.

TO PREPARE THE AÏOLI:

1. Using a mortar and pestle, crush together the garlic and salt. Add the potatoes, 1 at a time, and continue working until the mixture forms a thick paste.

2. Slowly whisk in the oil, creating an emulsion. The aïoli should be thick but not solid.

3. Transfer to a serving bowl. Serve surrounded with the cod, vegetables, and hard-boiled eggs.

BOUILLABAISSE

FOR THE *BOUILLABAISSE*:

1 recipe Fish Soup
(see recipe on p. 123)

20 small potatoes, peeled

4 pounds (1.82 kg) fish, such as Mediterranean sea bass, John Dory, red snapper, scorpion fish, ocean perch, rockfish, striped bass, or grouper

FOR THE *ROUILLE*:

3 cloves garlic

½ teaspoon sea salt

⅔ cup (158 mL) extra virgin olive oil

Pinch saffron threads, dissolved in 1 teaspoon water

FOR SERVING THE DISH:

16–20 slices bread, toasted

2 cups (200 g) grated Gruyère, for topping

In the past, Provençal fishermen would throw whatever catch they could not sell into a large pot of boiling water. They'd add some garlic and whatever spices they had on hand and wait! When the liquid started to reduce, they'd cry *"bouille baisse!"* (In English, "it's boiling down!") It was time to eat and the name of the soup was born. This dish evolved over time, and in the nineteenth century more expensive ingredients, such as saffron, were added. Today, *bouillabaisse* is emblematic of the city of Marseille, where the locals still heatedly debate what goes into it and who has the best recipe.

Traditionalists believe it is impossible to make real *bouillabaisse* away from the Mediterranean. In the spirit of rebellion, we set out to prove them wrong. After all, cooking is about using your imagination and combining diverse flavors to create a satisfying dish that tells a story. It is true that authentic (read: Marseillais) *bouillabaisse* draws its unique flavor from such Mediterranean species as the scorpion fish *(rascasse)*. But if you know your fish, or have a great fishmonger, you can make an intensely flavored *bouillabaisse* anywhere. To come close to recreating the Marseille classic, choose fish whose flavors resemble those found in the original dish.

Rascasse is the backbone of Marseille *bouillabaisse,* so start there (or another member of the *Scorpaenidae*

family). These days, you can find scorpion fish in ethnic fish stores—or instead, you can go with ocean perch, rockfish, and sculpin. Other delicious fish with similar textures that work well are ocean catfish, striped bass, sea bass, red snapper, grouper, blackfish, and tilefish.

Bouillabaisse is a party dish; you simply cannot make a great *bouillabaisse* for two people. So gather your friends and get ready for a feast! Make the Fish Soup (see recipe on p. 123) the day before using several different small fish for flavor. The day of the *bouillabaisse* party, chill some well-structured rosé and immerse yourself in the *art de vivre!*

A note on *rouille:* The issue of authentic *rouille* is not without controversy. As with *aïoli,* Provençals call the *rouille* that contains garlic, eggs, olive oil, and spices "Parisian *rouille."* (Not meant as a compliment!) The real *rouille* is more difficult to make, and time-consuming, but worth it. It starts with garlic and olive oil, but also includes potatoes cooked in the fish soup. It has a thicker consistency and has to be made by hand using a mortar and pestle. If you are making *bouillabaisse,* you need to go with tradition and make *rouille* the way François's grandmother used to. That is the only way!

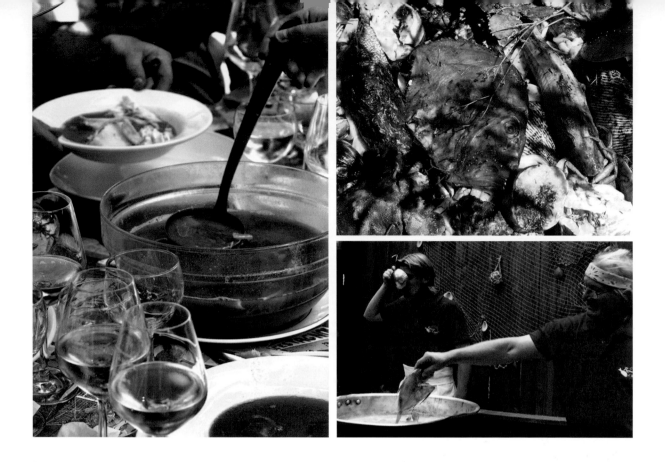

TO PREPARE THE *BOUILLABAISSE*:

1. In a large stockpot, warm the Fish Soup over medium-low heat and adjust the seasoning. Add the potatoes and cook for 5 minutes. Add the larger fish and the fish with firmer flesh and cook for 5 minutes. Add the smaller or softer-fleshed fish and cook for another 5 minutes.

2. Take out 4 of the potatoes and reserve them for the *rouille*.

TO PREPARE THE *ROUILLE*:

1. Using a mortar and pestle, crush together the garlic and salt. Add the 4 potatoes and continue working until the mixture forms a thick paste.

2. Slowly whisk in the oil, creating an emulsion. Add the saffron mixture halfway through. Transfer to a small serving bowl.

TO SERVE:

1. On a large platter, arrange the potatoes and fish. Transfer the soup to a large serving bowl. Place the toasted bread and the grated Gruyère into separate serving dishes. Bring everything to the table.

2. To serve each guest, place pieces of fish and potatoes in an individual soup bowl. Top with the Fish Soup. Instruct your guests to take slices of bread, slather them with *rouille*, top them with some Gruyère, and dunk them in the soup. When the bowls are empty, add more soup and continue the party!

OCTOPUS SALAD

Poulpes en Salade

4 cups (948 mL) fish or vegetable stock

2 pounds (908 g) octopus

4 green onions, chopped

2 tomatoes, diced

1 celery rib, with leaves, diced

15 sprigs chive, minced

¼ cup (32 g) chopped fresh parsley

2 cloves garlic, minced

Juice of ½ lime

Juice of ½ lemon

6 tablespoons (90 mL) fruity extra virgin olive oil

1 teaspoon hot sauce

½ teaspoon sea salt

Freshly ground black pepper, to taste

2 red endives, washed and leaves separated

Lemon and lime slices, for garnish

This fresh salad is the perfect light lunch or dinner with a chilled, minerally rosé.

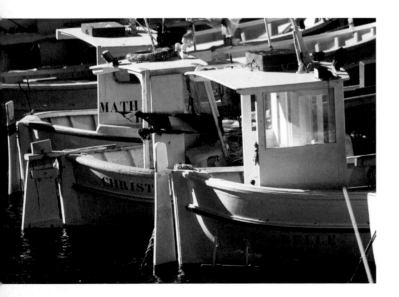

1. In a medium saucepan, bring the stock to a boil over medium-high heat. Add the octopus. Reduce the heat to low and cook for 20 minutes. Remove from the heat, cover, and set aside to cool to room temperature.

2. Once cool, drain the octopus and chop into bite-sized pieces.

3. In a medium mixing bowl, combine the octopus, green onions, tomatoes, celery, chives, and parsley. Set aside.

4. In a small mixing bowl, combine the garlic, citrus juices, oil, hot sauce, salt, and a grind of the black pepper.

5. In a salad bowl, arrange the endive leaves in a circle and add the octopus and vegetables. Dress with the garlic–citrus mixture and serve chilled with slices of lemon and lime.

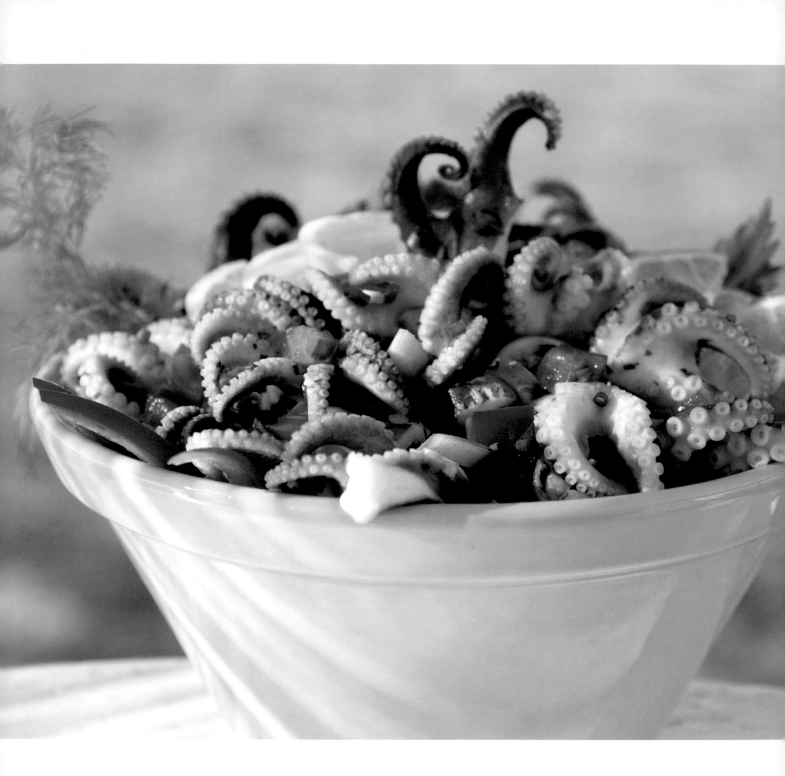

OCTOPUS STEW WITH ROSÉ

Daube de Poulpe au Vin Rosé

— YIELD: 4 SERVINGS —

FOR THE *BOUQUET GARNI*:

3–4 sprigs fresh parsley

3 sprigs fresh thyme

2 sprigs fresh savory

1 sprig fresh rosemary

FOR THE STEW:

2 quarts (1.90 L) water

2 pounds (908 g) baby octopus

½ cup (119 mL) Cognac, whiskey, or Armagnac

4 sprigs fresh parsley

4 sprigs thyme

1 fresh bay leaf

½ teaspoon whole fennel seeds

½ teaspoon plus pinch sea salt, divided

Freshly ground black pepper, to taste

4 ounces (114 g) pancetta, cubed (about 1 cup)

1 large yellow onion, chopped

2 medium tomatoes, peeled, seeded, and diced (see Cooks' Note on p. 101 for peeling instructions)

4 cloves garlic, thinly sliced

2 cups rosé

2 cups hot water

This delectable stew is great served over rice, and pairs well with the rosé used to make it. *Santé!*

TO PREPARE THE *BOUQUET GARNI*:

1. Tie the herbs together with a string, or wrap together in cheesecloth. Set aside.

TO PREPARE THE STEW:

1. In a medium pot, bring the water to a boil over medium-high heat. Add the octopus and cook for 2 to 3 minutes. Drain and set aside to cool to room temperature. Once cool, cut the octopus into bite-sized pieces.

2. In a medium mixing bowl, combine the octopus, Cognac, parsley, thyme, bay leaf, fennel seeds, the pinch of salt, and a grind of the black pepper. Refrigerate for 5 to 6 hours.

3. Drain the octopus, discarding the herbs and reserving the liquid.

4. In a medium sauté pan, warm the pancetta over medium heat until the fat starts to render. Add the onion and cook for 5 to 7 minutes. Add the tomatoes, garlic, and octopus and cook for 3 to 4 minutes, until the liquid from the tomatoes has evaporated.

5. Add the reserved liquid, wine, hot water, *bouquet garni*, and the remaining ½ teaspoon of salt. Bring to a boil, reduce the heat to low, and cook for 1½ hours. Remove from the heat.

6. Remove and discard the *bouquet garni*. Transfer to a serving bowl and serve hot.

MUSSELS À LA PROVENÇAL

Moules à la Provençale

— YIELD: 4 SERVINGS —

2 pounds (908 g) mussels

½ cup (119 mL) water

2 tablespoons extra virgin olive oil

2 shallots, finely chopped

1 teaspoon whole coriander seeds

1 cup (237 mL) dry white wine

1 teaspoon chopped fresh thyme

1 fresh bay leaf

4 ripe tomatoes, peeled, seeded, and chopped (see Cooks' Note)

1 clove garlic, minced

Juice of ½ lemon

½ teaspoon lemon zest

Sea salt and freshly ground black pepper, to taste

1 spring onion, finely chopped

1. In a large sauté pan, cook the mussels in the water until they open over medium-high heat. Remove from the heat and strain, reserving the cooking water. Remove and discard half of each shell. Place the mussels on a large plate with half of the reserved cooking water and refrigerate. Reserve the remaining cooking water.

2. In a medium sauté pan, warm the oil over medium heat. Add the shallots and coriander seeds and cook for 5 to 7 minutes, until the shallots start to brown. Add the white wine, thyme, bay leaf, and the remaining reserved cooking water and cook for 3 to 4 minutes, until the liquid is reduced by about ⅓. Add the chopped tomatoes, garlic, lemon juice and zest, a sprinkling of salt, and a grind of the black pepper. Reduce the heat to low and cook for 10 minutes. Remove from the heat and set aside to cool.

3. On a serving platter, arrange the mussels on the half shell in a single layer. Place 1 tablespoon of the tomato mixture and some of the chopped spring onion onto each mussel. Cover the platter with plastic wrap and refrigerate for 2 hours. Serve cold.

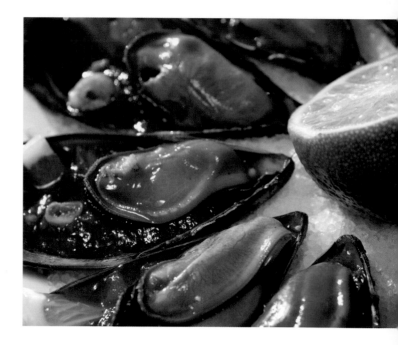

COOKS' NOTE: *To peel the tomatoes, cut an X on the bottom of each one, then submerge in boiling water for 30 seconds (to loosen the skin). Drain immediately and shock with cold water, then set aside to cool. Once cool enough to handle, peel the skin.*

POTATO *PISSALADIÈRE* WITH SARDINES AND ANCHOVIES

YIELD: 4 SERVINGS

FOR THE ONION *CONFIT*:

3 tablespoons (45 mL) extra virgin olive oil

2 medium red onions, quartered and sliced very thinly

¼ cup (59 mL) dry red wine

I whole star anise

I tablespoon honey

I tablespoon red wine vinegar

3 whole cardamom seeds

½ teaspoon salt

¼ teaspoon crushed fennel seeds

Freshly ground black pepper, to taste

FOR THE POTATO *GALETTE*:

2 tablespoons extra virgin olive oil

2 tablespoons butter

2 medium russet potatoes, peeled and grated

Salt and freshly ground black pepper, to taste

FOR THE *PISSALADIÈRE*:

2 small, fresh sardine fillets, halved

4 tablespoons (59 mL) extra virgin olive oil, divided

Juice of ½ lemon

2 teaspoons chopped fresh parsley

Pinch ground *piment d'Espelette*, unsmoked hot paprika, cayenne, pimento, or Aleppo pepper

Salt and freshly ground black pepper, to taste

4 anchovy fillets in oil

2 dried tomatoes, quartered lengthwise

¼ cup (36 g) black olives, pitted

I fresh artichoke, quartered

I cup (30 g) salad greens

¼ cup (7 g) edible flowers, for garnish

Chef Lionel Levy, the executive chef of the Intercontinental Hotel in Marseille and a true master of Provençal cuisine, has reimagined the traditional *pissaladière* (see p. 136 for that version) to give it a different texture and new flavors. Pair this sophisticated starter with a dry, aromatic rosé, which goes perfectly with exotic flavors.

TO PREPARE THE *CONFIT*:

1. In a medium sauté pan, warm the oil over medium-high heat. Add the onion and cook for 3 to 5 minutes, until the liquid is released. Add the wine and continue cooking for 1 to 2 minutes, until the alcohol has evaporated.

2. Reduce the heat to very low. Add the star anise, honey, vinegar, spices, salt, and a grind of the black pepper. Stir well. Cook for 2 hours, adding a little water if necessary to prevent the onions from burning. Remove from the heat, remove and discard the star anise and cardamom seeds, adjust the seasoning to taste, and set aside. The onion *confit* can be made up to 2 days ahead and refrigerated.

TO PREPARE THE POTATO *GALETTE*:

1. In a medium nonstick sauté pan, warm the oil and butter over medium-high heat. Add the potatoes, sprinkle with the salt and black pepper, and cook for 2 to 3 minutes. Reduce the heat to medium and continue cooking until the *galette* starts to brown and can be easily pulled away from the side of the pan. With a large spatula, flip the *galette* and cook for 7 to 8 minutes, until the other side is golden brown. Remove from the heat and set aside.

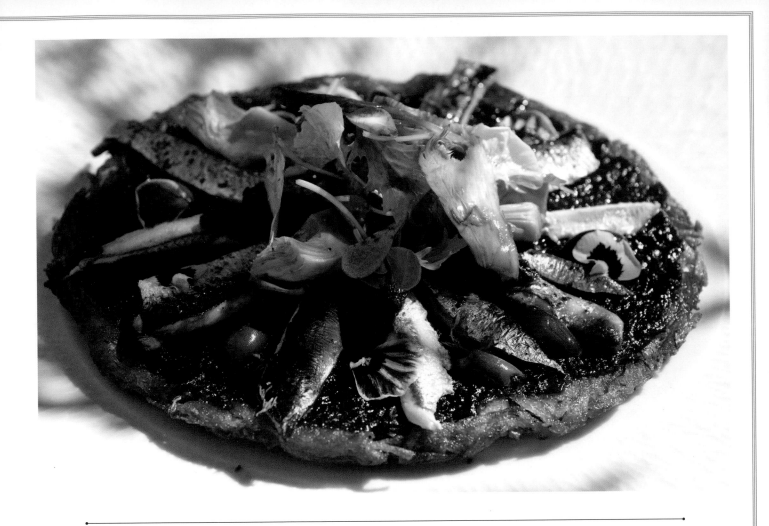

TO PREPARE THE *PISSALADIÈRE:*

1. Preheat the broiler to medium and set an oven rack to the center position.

2. Place the sardine fillets in an ovenproof dish and drizzle with 2 tablespoons of the oil and the lemon juice. Sprinkle with the parsley and *piment d'Espelette* and season to taste with the salt and black pepper. Cook under the broiler for 2 to 3 minutes. Remove from the oven and set aside.

3. Place the potato *galette* on a large serving plate. Spread the onion *confit* evenly over the *galette*. Top with the anchovy fillets and sardine halves, alternating them in a fanlike manner that radiates out from the center of the *galette*. Arrange the tomatoes and olives on top and add the artichoke quarters. Place the salad greens in the middle of the *galette*.

4. Drizzle the salad greens with the oil and season with the salt and black pepper. Sprinkle with the edible flowers and serve warm or at room temperature.

SALTED COD WITH FENNEL, TOMATOES, AÏOLI, AND SAFFRON

Morue au Fenouil, Tomates, Aïoli, et Safran

YIELD: 4 SERVINGS

Pinch saffron threads

3 tablespoons (45 mL) extra virgin olive oil

2 medium yellow onions, chopped

Pinch sea salt, plus more to taste

2 bulbs fennel, halved lengthwise and sliced

1 clove garlic, minced

1 fresh bay leaf

1 cup (237 mL) dry white wine

½ teaspoon orange zest

5 ripe tomatoes, peeled and halved (see Cooks' Note on p. 101 for peeling instructions)

1 cup (237 mL) chicken or vegetable stock

1 teaspoon chopped fresh thyme

2 pounds (908 g) salted cod, soaked in cold water for at least 24 hours, then cut into 1-inch (2.5-cm) pieces

¾ cup (108 g) black olives, pitted and chopped

Freshly ground black pepper, to taste

1 recipe *Aïoli* (see recipe on p. 95, optional)

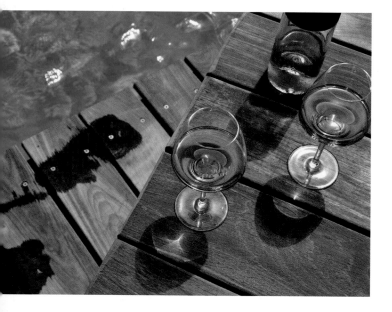

1. In a large sauté pan, warm the saffron threads over medium heat. Add the oil and stir. Add the onions and the pinch of salt and cook for 7 to 8 minutes.

2. Add the fennel and cook for 5 to 7 minutes. Add the garlic and bay leaf and cook for another minute. Add the wine and cook for another 2 to 3 minutes, until the wine has reduced by ⅓. Add the orange zest and the tomatoes. Add the stock and thyme, reduce the heat to low, and cook for 15 minutes.

3. Add the salted cod and olives, making sure the fish is covered with liquid, and cook for 6 to 7 minutes. Season to taste with the salt and black pepper. Remove and discard the bay leaf. Serve warm, with *Aïoli* on the side, if using.

SARDINES WITH CITRUS, MARSEILLE STYLE

Sardines aux Citrons Comme à Marseille

8 sardine fillets

Juice of 2 large lemons

Juice of 2 limes

1 teaspoon grated fresh ginger (optional)

Sea salt and freshly ground black pepper, to taste

1 small yellow onion, sliced very thinly

1 teaspoon whole coriander seeds, for garnish

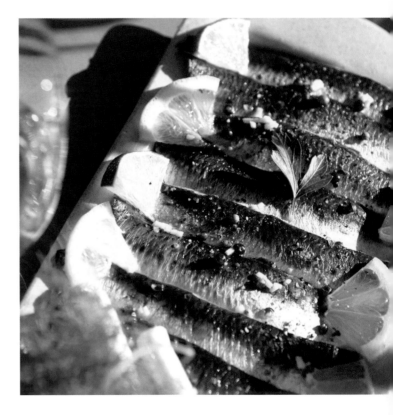

In Marseille, and along the coast more generally, the sardine is an institution, cooked in a variety of ways or simply marinated in lemon and lime juice. Of course, this dish starts at the market—and if you are lucky, at the fresh fish market—because the sardines need to be super fresh. Ask the fishmonger to fillet and debone the sardines. The rest is easy: all you need is an aromatic and lively rosé from Côtes de Provence, preferably one that comes from the seaboard, which will match the saltiness of the sardines and the zing of the citrus. Pour your friends a glass as an aperitif and the party is ready to start.

1. In a shallow bowl, combine the sardines, citrus juices, and ginger, if using. Season to taste with the salt and black pepper and toss.

2. On a platter, layer some of the onion slices. Arrange the sardines in a single layer, drizzle with the juices from the bowl, and add some more onion slices.

3. Adjust the seasoning, garnish with the coriander seeds, and serve cold.

BERRY MILLE-FEUILLES WITH ORANGE COOKIES

Mille-Feuilles de Tuiles à l'Orange aux Fruits Rouges

YIELD: 6 SERVINGS

FOR THE ORANGE COOKIES:

2 cups (224 g) finely chopped almonds

1 cup (192 g) granulated sugar

⅔ cup (84 g) all-purpose flour

½ cup (114 g) butter, softened (1 stick)

⅓ cup (79 mL) orange juice

Zest of 1 orange

1 tablespoon Grand Marnier liqueur

FOR THE CHANTILLY:

2 cups (474 mL) whole or 2% milk

1 vanilla bean, cut open

5 egg yolks

½ cup (96 g) granulated sugar

2 tablespoons cornstarch

1 cup (237 mL) whipping cream

FOR ASSEMBLING THE DISH:

1½ cups (216 g) small strawberries

1½ cups (216 g) red raspberries

1½ (341 g) cups blueberries

12 fresh mint leaves

This beautiful dessert seduces the eye before it even gets to the palate. The varied colors and flavors call for a fresh, lively, and nuanced rosé with berry flavors. Choose one from Côtes de Provence for an ideal pairing.

TO PREPARE THE COOKIES:

1. Preheat the oven to 350°F (180°C). Line 2 11 × 17-inch (27.5 × 43-cm) baking sheets with parchment paper. Set aside.

2. In a large mixing bowl, combine all the ingredients and stir well. Using a tablespoon, scoop out the dough and place dollops of it 1½ inches (3.8 cm) apart on the prepared baking sheet.

3. Bake for 15 to 18 minutes, until golden. Remove from the oven. Cool on a wire rack.

TO PREPARE THE CHANTILLY:

1. In a medium saucepan, combine the milk and vanilla over medium heat. Bring to a boil. Remove from the heat.

2. In a medium mixing bowl, beat together the egg yolks and sugar until the mixture is thick and pale. Add the cornstarch and slowly temper in the milk–vanilla mixture, 1 cup (237 mL) at a time, making sure not to scramble the eggs.

3. Return the mixture to the saucepan and cook over low heat, stirring constantly, until the pastry cream comes to a boil and thickens. Remove from the heat.

4. Transfer the pastry cream to a bowl and cover with plastic wrap (make sure the wrap touches the surface of the pastry cream, in order to prevent a crust from forming). Set aside to cool to room temperature.

5. In a very cold bowl, whip the whipping cream. Add the whipped cream to the pastry cream and stir well, creating a Chantilly.

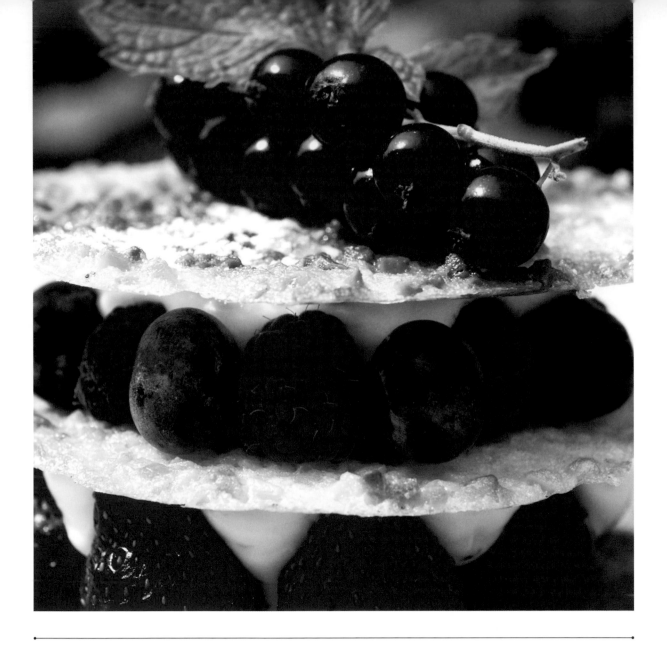

TO ASSEMBLE THE DISH:

1. Place 6 of the cookies on a large platter. Arrange the strawberries in a circle on each cookie, leaving 1 inch (2.5 cm) in the center of each cookie empty. Fill the empty space with the Chantilly. Cover with another cookie and make a circle with raspberries and blueberries. Fill the center with the Chantilly. Cover with a third cookie and decorate with more fruit and 2 mint leaves. Serve immediately.

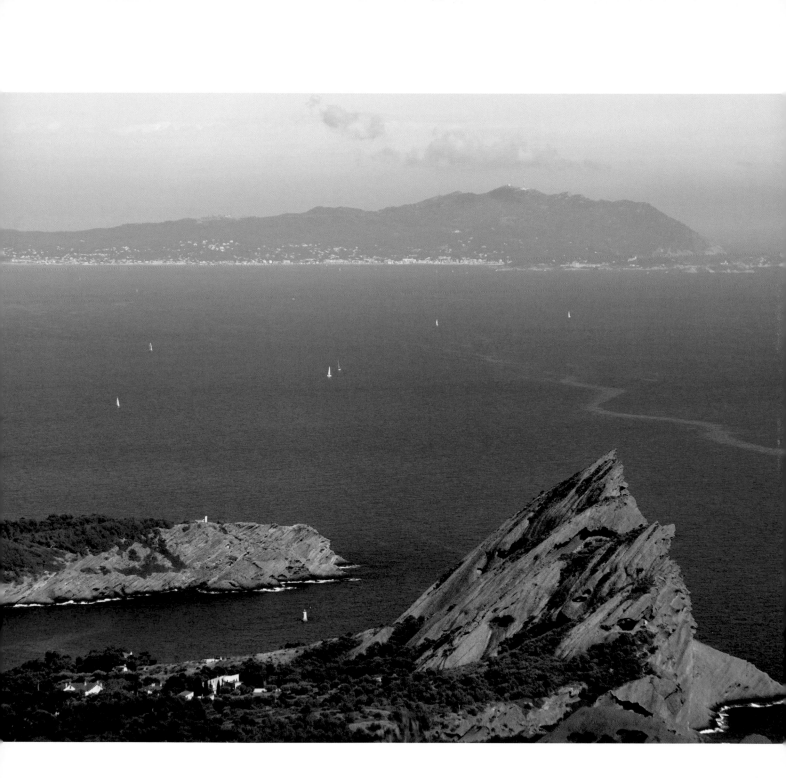

La Côte Varoise

LA CÔTE VAROISE, THE STRETCH OF LAND BETWEEN MARSEILLE and Cannes, has a varied geography and an equally varied and interesting cuisine. The cooking differs both from one seaside town to the next as well as between the coast and the inland area.

The coast abounds in flavorful Mediterranean fare, including colorful small fish like red mullet, sea bass, sea bream, langoustines, *petits poissons de roche, calamars, oursins,* and *fruits de mer* (small rockfish, calamari, sea urchins, and other seafood). These varied sea creatures give a unique flavor to the cooking in towns like Saint-Tropez and the other, smaller villages that dot the coast. And then there are the Hyères islands: le Levant, Port-Cros (a national park), and Porquerolles, the biggest island, where what's on the menu depends on what the fishermen bring in that morning. Cooks might not be able to plan exactly what they will cook that day, but they know it will be delicious, because the clear Mediterranean waters are home to the most delicious fish.

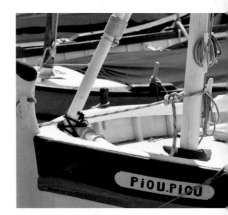

Flavorful vegetables—tomatoes, zucchini, purple artichokes, eggplant, and wild asparagus—complete the palette of flavors of this area. They are prepared simply: Young, crisp artichokes may be served raw, thinly sliced, and drizzled with extra virgin olive oil. Peppers are grilled and served with a little of their own juice, extra virgin olive oil, and garlic. Simple and supremely delicious! Because when you start with fresh, flavorful ingredients, you do not need to

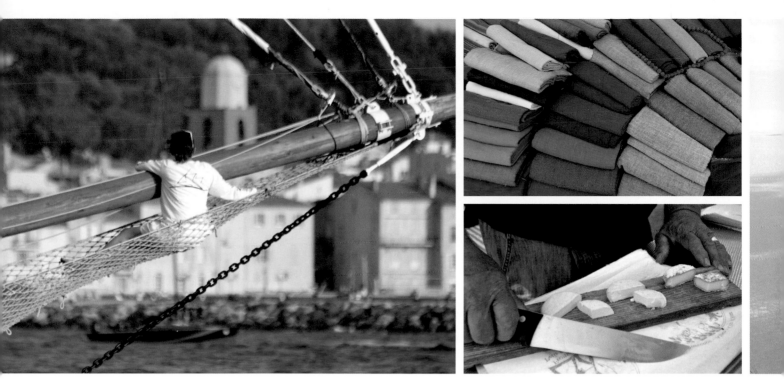

do much. Further inland, the vegetables might be cooked over low heat for a longer time, a method that concentrates the flavors and gives richness to the dish. On the coast, grilling and quick cooking methods are more common. And, of course, the dishes are flavored with fresh aromatic herbs: rosemary, basil, and savory. This gives them additional flavor without altering their essence. Once again, Provence dazzles with simplicity and extraordinary flavors!

Going inland, the landscape changes quickly, and the Maures, the chain of coastal mountains that runs from Hyères to Fréjus, is home to chestnut forests, the fruits of which have been part of the local economy for centuries. The importance of chestnut production might have diminished over the last century, but there are still passionate producers who create delicious products from the chestnuts in this area, which are recognized as being of particularly high quality.

The mountain village of Collobrières is home to several producers of chestnut delicacies, from chestnut cream and candied chestnuts to flavorful ice

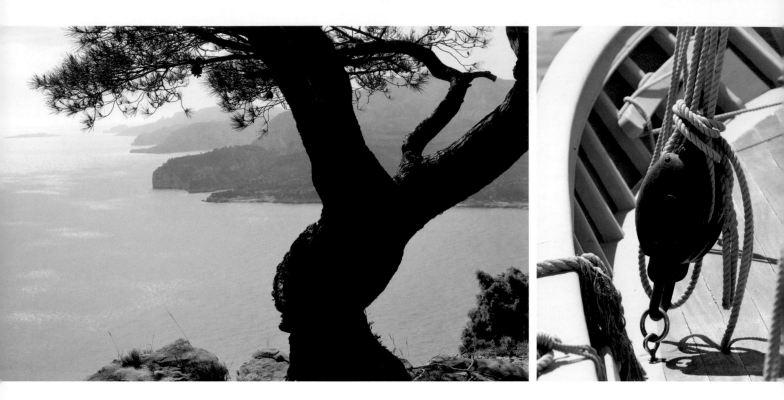

cream. Chestnuts are harvested between mid-September and November, and they are available fresh at the local markets until February. Chestnut products, such as chestnut flour, cooked and peeled chestnuts, and chestnut purée are available year-round and find their way into many dishes. Poultry, pork, and veal pair well with chestnuts, but so do fish such as haddock, both fresh and smoked. And of course, chestnut flour is used in cakes and cookies, and chestnut purée is a tasty sweet treat all by itself. The hard-working Provençal bees also make delicious honey from chestnut flowers. Dark and intense in flavor, this honey is a perfect pairing for chèvre, especially aged varieties.

Another product typical of the area is the local fig, *figue de solliès*. It has been recognized with an AOC label since 2006. These purple delicacies have a dense and soft flesh and a flavor balanced with sweetness and acidity. Enjoyed fresh in the summer or in *confitures* (jams) year-round, they find their way into many Provençal desserts, including simple preparations like roasted figs drizzled with honey.

GRILLED PEPPERS IN EXTRA VIRGIN OLIVE OIL

Poivrons au Four, Marinés à l'Huile d'Olive

YIELD: 12 SERVINGS

2 red bell peppers

2 yellow bell peppers

2 orange bell peppers

3 garlic cloves, minced

3 tablespoons (24 g) chopped fresh parsley

3 tablespoons (45 mL) extra virgin olive oil

1 teaspoon sea salt, plus more to taste

Freshly ground black pepper, to taste

6 anchovy fillets (optional)

The quality of this dish depends on the quality of the main ingredient, so choose peppers that are ripe and you will enjoy lots of flavor and a hint of sweetness.

The powerful pepper is like an old childhood friend of Provence rosé, which complements perfectly with its aroma, flavor, and freshness.

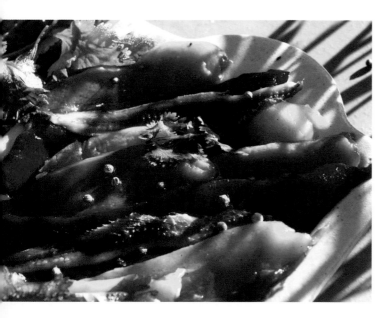

1. Preheat the broiler on high.

2. Place the peppers on a baking sheet lined with aluminum foil and roast them under the broiler for 7 to 8 minutes, turning after 3 to 4 minutes so they do not burn. (The peppers should be well roasted on all sides.) Remove from the oven.

3. Place the peppers in a brown paper bag and let them rest at room temperature for 10 to 15 minutes.

4. Using a cloth, rub the peppers vigorously. The skins should slide off easily. Slice the peppers into ½-inch (13-mm) slices. Discard the peppers' skins, stems, and the seeds and reserve the juice.

5. Strain the juice into a small bowl. Add the garlic, parsley, and oil, and combine.

6. On a serving platter, arrange a single layer of peppers. Drizzle some of the pepper juice mixture over the sliced peppers and sprinkle with the 1 teaspoon salt, adding more to taste, and black pepper. Repeat with the remaining peppers.

7. Set aside at room temperature for several hours or overnight. Before serving, add the anchovy fillets, if using.

RED MULLET *BRANDADE*
Brandade de Rougets

2 cups (474 mL) whole or 2% milk

⅔ pound (312 g) red mullet fillets, divided

4 garlic cloves

I medium potato, cubed

2 cups (474 mL) water

¼ teaspoon sea salt, plus more to taste

Freshly ground black pepper, to taste

I tablespoon extra virgin olive oil, plus more for drizzling

This typical Provençal dish is the perfect bite to start a meal alongside a glass of mineral-flavored, chilled rosé.

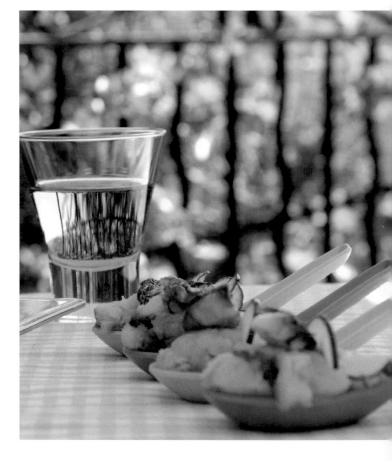

1. In a small saucepan, bring the milk to a boil over medium heat. Add ½ pound (227 g) of the mullet and the garlic to the saucepan and cook for 6 to 8 minutes. Strain the fish and set aside, reserving the milk.

2. In another small saucepan, combine the potato, water, and salt. Bring to a boil and cook until the potato is fork tender. Remove from the heat.

3. Transfer the potato to the bowl of a food processor or blender. Add the cooked mullet and enough of the milk to process the mixture to a nearly smooth texture, creating a *brandade*. Season to taste with the salt and black pepper.

4. In a small sauté pan, warm the oil over medium heat. Add the remaining mullet fillets and cook for 2 to 3 minutes per side, until they are flaky. Remove from the heat and, when cool enough to handle, cut into ½-inch (13-mm) pieces.

5. To assemble the dish, place a little of the *brandade* on a spoon. Add a piece of fried red mullet and drizzle with a little of the oil. Serve warm.

GRILLED RED MULLET WITH *PISTOU RATATOUILLE* AND GARLIC POTATOES

Grillade de Rouget avec Ratatouille au Pistou et Pommes de Terre Fondantes à l'Ail

— YIELD: 4 SERVINGS —

FOR THE *PISTOU*:

1 cup (25 g) fresh basil

3–4 tablespoons (45–59 mL) extra virgin olive oil

Sea salt and freshly ground black pepper, to taste

FOR THE *RATATOUILLE*:

5 tablespoons (75 mL) extra virgin olive oil, divided

1 small eggplant, diced

1 medium zucchini, diced

1 small red bell pepper, diced

1 small green bell pepper, diced

1 small yellow bell pepper, diced

1 medium yellow onion, diced

2 cloves garlic

1 medium ripe tomato, seeded and chopped

Sea salt and freshly ground black pepper, to taste

FOR THE GARLIC POTATOES:

2 large Yukon gold potatoes, peeled

1 quart (948 mL) water

2 cloves garlic

1 teaspoon sea salt, plus more to taste

FOR THE FISH:

8 red mullet fillets, skin on

1 cup (237 mL) extra virgin olive oil, plus more for brushing

12–16 fresh basil leaves, for garnish

Chef Thierry Thiercelin of Hôtel Villa Belrose, a Relais & Châteaux hotel in Gassin Saint-Tropez, combines traditional Provençal ingredients in this modernized, sophisticated dish. Pair with a dry, mineral rosé from the coast of Provence.

TO PREPARE THE *PISTOU*:

1. In a blender or the bowl of a food processor, combine the basil and oil and pulse to chop. Season to taste with the salt and black pepper and set aside.

TO PREPARE THE *RATATOUILLE*:

1. In a medium sauté pan, warm 2 tablespoons of the oil over medium-high heat. Add the eggplant and cook, stirring occasionally, for 12 to 15 minutes. Transfer to a plate lined with paper towels.

2. In the same sauté pan, warm 1 tablespoon of the oil. Add the zucchini and cook for 8 to 10 minutes. Transfer to a second plate lined with paper towels.

3. In the same sauté pan, warm another tablespoon of the oil. Add the peppers and cook for 7 to 8 minutes. Transfer to a third plate lined with paper towels.

4. In the same sauté pan, warm the remaining tablespoon of oil. Add the onions, and cook, stirring occasionally, for 10 minutes. Add the garlic, stir well, and cook for 1 minute.

5. Return all of the cooked vegetables to the sauté pan and stir well. Add the tomatoes and cook for 2 to 3 minutes, until they release their liquid. Remove from the heat and add all but ½ tablespoon of the *pistou*. Season to taste with the salt and black pepper and set aside.

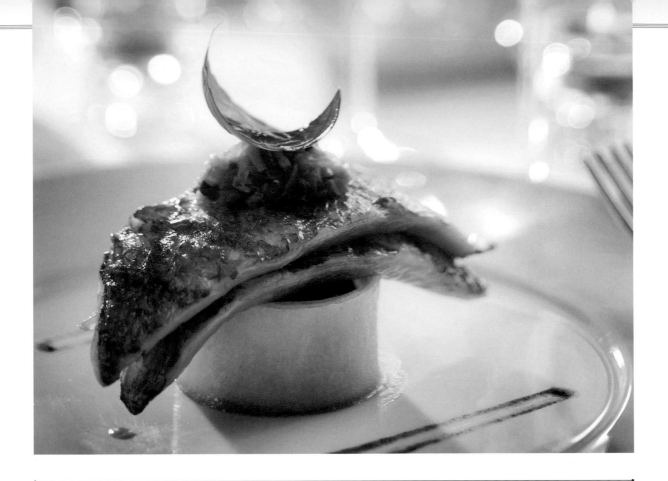

TO PREPARE THE GARLIC POTATOES:

1. Cut two 1½-inch (3.8-cm) rounds out of each potato (remove the rounded ends). Scoop out the inside of the potato to obtain a ¼-inch-thick (6-mm-thick) ring.

2. In a medium stockpot, bring the water, garlic, and salt to a boil over medium-high heat. Add the potatoes and cook until done but not too soft. Remove from the heat, drain, and set aside.

TO PREPARE THE FISH:

1. Brush the red mullet fillets with some of the oil.

2. In a shallow sauté pan, warm the 1 cup (237 mL) of oil over low heat.

3. On a stovetop griddle, grill the fillets, skin-side down, for 2 minutes over medium-high heat.

4. Remove the fillets from the griddle and submerge them in the warm oil. Cook for 1 minute. Remove from the heat.

TO ASSEMBLE THE DISH:

1. Place a potato ring on each of 4 plates and fill the inside with the *ratatouille*. Place 2 fillets on top of each potato ring and garnish with some *ratatouille*, fresh basil, and the remaining *pistou*. Serve warm.

BARBEQUED MUSSELS

Brasucade

FOR THE AROMATIC BASE:

1 cup (237 mL) dry white wine

1 medium onion, chopped

⅓ cup (79 mL) extra virgin olive oil

¼ cup (32 g) chopped fresh parsley

1 clove garlic, crushed

2 sprigs fresh thyme

1 sprig fresh rosemary

FOR THE MUSSELS:

4 pounds (1.82 kg) mussels

Sea salt and freshly ground black pepper, to taste

A warm summer night, a gathering of friends under the clear Provence sky, a chilled, crisp rosé—it's *brasucade* time, of course. The fire is hot, the mussels are ready, and everyone is huddling around to get a taste fresh from the pan. *Brasucade* is a typical outdoor dish, cooked over an open flame. If you are cooking indoors, use a wok or a large frying pan, and serve the mussels straight out of the pan.

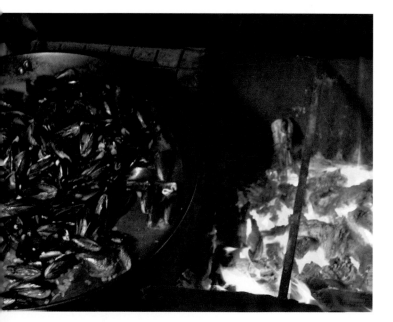

TO PREPARE THE AROMATIC BASE:

1. In a large mixing bowl, combine the aromatic base ingredients. Cover with plastic wrap and refrigerate for several hours or overnight.

TO PREPARE THE MUSSELS:

1. Preheat the grill.

2. In a large heatproof pan placed on the grill, warm the aromatic base for 5 minutes. Add the mussels and cook until they open. Remove from the heat.

3. Remove the mussels from the pan and place them in a serving bowl. (Discard any unopened mussels.)

4. Season to taste with the salt and black pepper and serve immediately.

COOKS' NOTE: *Burnt fingers are common when one serves brasucade, but that's fully expected. A well-chilled rosé helps cool things off.*

RATATOUILLE

YIELD: 10–12 SERVINGS

9 tablespoons (135 mL) extra virgin olive oil, divided

1 medium eggplant, cut into ½-inch (13-mm) dice (about 4 cups [328 g])

3 medium zucchini, cut into ½-inch (13-mm) dice (about 4 cups [496 g])

1 red, orange, or yellow bell pepper, cut into ½-inch (13-mm) dice (about 1 cup [150 g])

1 medium yellow onion, cut into ½-inch (13-mm) dice (about 1½ cups [171 g])

2 cloves garlic, minced

3 large (or 4 medium) ripe tomatoes, cut into ½-inch (13-mm) dice (about 4 cups [384 g])

1½ teaspoons sea salt

1 tablespoon chopped fresh thyme

6 leaves fresh basil, torn into small pieces

*R*atatouille may be the most famous Provençal dish. And maybe because of that, it has as many variations as there are cooks. In this unusual (heretical, we like to say) version, we use peppers, in addition to eggplant and zucchini, to add a texture and flavor dimension and to make the dish more interesting. The important thing about *ratatouille* is to cook the vegetables separately first, and then combine everything into a whole that is always more delicious than the sum of its parts.

1. In a large sauté pan, warm 3 tablespoons (45 mL) of the oil over medium-high heat. Add the eggplant and cook, stirring occasionally, for 12 to 15 minutes, until browned on all sides. Transfer the eggplant to a large plate lined with paper towels.

2. Reduce the heat to medium. In the same sauté pan, warm 2 tablespoons of the oil. Add the zucchini and cook, stirring occasionally, for 10 to 12 minutes, until the zucchini are crisp on the outside. Transfer the zucchini to a large plate lined with paper towels.

3. In the same sauté pan, warm 1 tablespoon of the oil. Add the pepper and cook, stirring occasionally, for 7 to 8 minutes, until the pepper starts to soften. Transfer the pepper to a large plate lined with paper towels.

4. In the same sauté pan, warm the remaining 3 tablespoons (45 mL) of the oil. Add the onion and cook, stirring occasionally, for 10 to 12 minutes, until softened. Add the garlic, stir well, and cook for another 1 to 2 minutes, until the garlic releases its aroma. Add the tomatoes, stir well, and continue to cook for another 7 to 8 minutes, until the tomatoes release their liquid. Add the eggplant, zucchini, pepper, and the salt, stir well, and cook for 10 to 12 minutes. Add the thyme, stir well, and continue cooking for 1 minute. Remove from the heat.

5. Add the basil and stir well. Adjust the salt to taste.

6. Transfer to a serving bowl and serve warm or at room temperature.

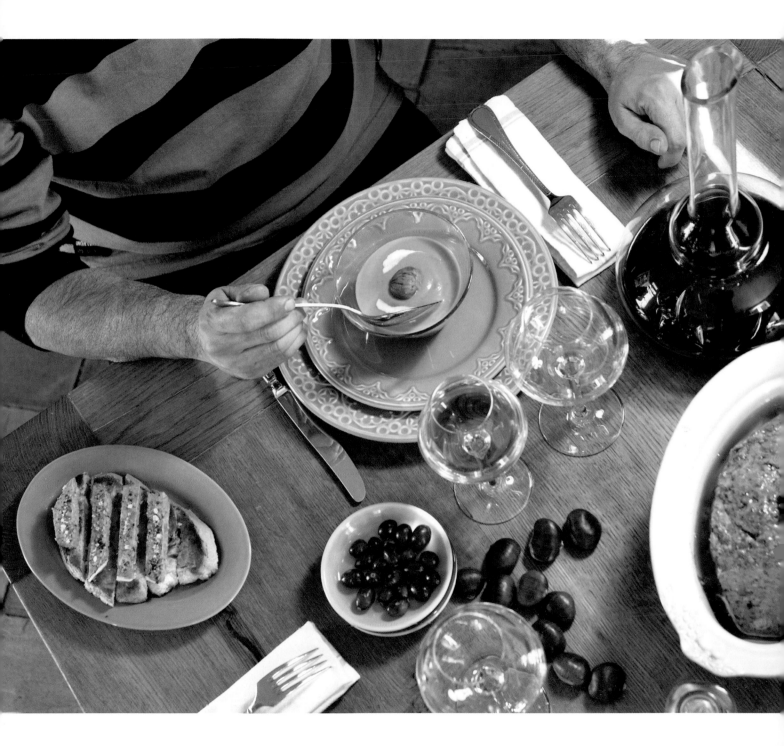

PUMPKIN SOUP WITH CHESTNUTS

Velouté de Potiron aux Châtaignes

YIELD: 4–6 SERVINGS

2 tablespoons butter

1 shallot, minced

2 pounds (908 g) pumpkin, cut into 1-inch (2.5-cm) squares (about 5 cups)

4 cups (948 mL) chicken broth

1 cup (143 g) cooked chestnuts, plus more for garnish

Pinch ground nutmeg

1 teaspoon sea salt, plus more to taste

Freshly ground black pepper, to taste

¾ cup (178 mL) heavy cream

Rich, velvety, and satisfying, this soup is great for cooler weather. It is the perfect Provençal comfort food.

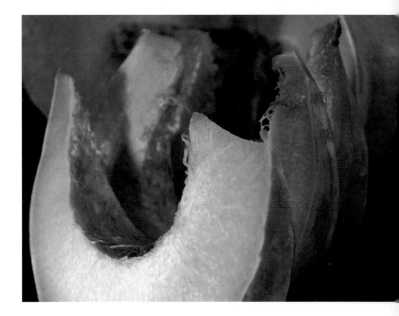

1. In a medium saucepan, warm the butter over medium heat. Add the shallot and cook for 5 minutes, until softened. Add the pumpkin, chicken broth, the 1 cup (143 g) of chestnuts, nutmeg, salt, and a grind of the black pepper. Raise the heat to medium-high and bring to a boil. Reduce the heat to medium-low and cook for 20 minutes. Remove from the heat.

2. Process the mixture briefly with an immersion blender (or transfer to a blender for processing).

3. Add the heavy cream and stir well. Adjust the seasoning to taste.

4. Transfer to serving bowls and serve hot, garnished with some of the chestnuts.

TIAN À LA PROVENÇALE

YIELD: 4 SERVINGS

FOR THE CARAMELIZED ONIONS:

¼ cup (59 mL) olive oil

2 large onions, thinly sliced

I fresh bay leaf

2 sprigs fresh thyme

Pinch granulated sugar

Kosher salt and freshly ground black pepper, to taste

FOR THE VEGETABLES:

I medium zucchini, sliced in ¹⁄₁₆-inch (1.6-mm) rounds

I medium eggplant, sliced into ¹⁄₁₆-inch (1.6-mm) rounds

I medium yellow squash, sliced into ¹⁄₁₆-inch (1.6-mm) rounds

4 Roma tomatoes, sliced into ¹⁄₁₆-inch (1.6-mm) rounds

½ teaspoon minced garlic

2 teaspoons extra virgin olive oil

⅛ teaspoon fresh thyme leaves

Kosher salt and freshly ground black pepper, to taste

FOR THE GARNISH:

Extra virgin olive oil, for drizzling

2 tablespoons chiffonaded fresh basil

I teaspoon ground *piment d'Espelette*, unsmoked hot paprika, cayenne, pimento, or Aleppo pepper

I head roasted garlic

This recipe from Chef Mathias Gervais, executive chef for The Setai Hotel in Miami Beach, Florida, is for a layered vegetable casserole, a typical Provençal dish.

TO PREPARE THE CARAMELIZED ONIONS:

1. In a large sauté pan, warm the oil over medium heat. Add the onions, bay leaf, thyme sprigs, and sugar and toss. Reduce the heat to low, cover, and cook, stirring occasionally, for 10 minutes, until the onions are golden in color.

2. Increase the heat to medium-high and brown the onions, stirring constantly, for 10 minutes. Remove from the heat. Season to taste with the salt and black pepper. Remove and discard the bay leaf and thyme.

3. Transfer the caramelized onions to a cast-iron casserole dish, spreading them evenly over the bottom. Set aside.

TO PREPARE THE VEGETABLES:

1. Preheat the oven to 275°F (140°C).

2. Arrange the vegetables as shown in the photo, alternating them for variety.

3. In a small mixing bowl, mix the garlic, oil, and thyme leaves. Season to taste with the salt and black pepper. Drizzle the mixture over the vegetables.

4. Cover the casserole dish with aluminum foil, crimping the edges to seal well. Bake 2 hours, or until the vegetables are tender when tested with a paring knife. Uncover and bake for 30 more minutes. If the vegetables start to brown, lightly cover the dish with aluminum foil. Remove from the oven.

5. If excess liquid remains in the casserole dish, place it over medium heat on the stove and cook until the liquid has reduced. Remove from the heat. Allow to cool to room temperature. Cover and refrigerate for up to 2 days.

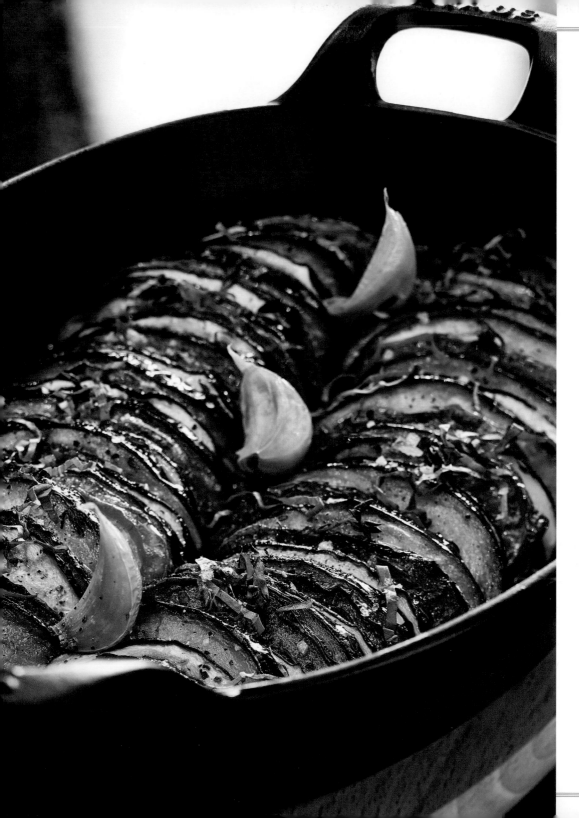

TO SERVE THE DISH:

1. This dish can be served cold or reheated in the oven at 350°F (180°C) for 30 minutes, until warm.

2. Finish with a drizzle of the oil. Garnish with the basil, *piment d'Espelette*, and roasted garlic cloves. Serve.

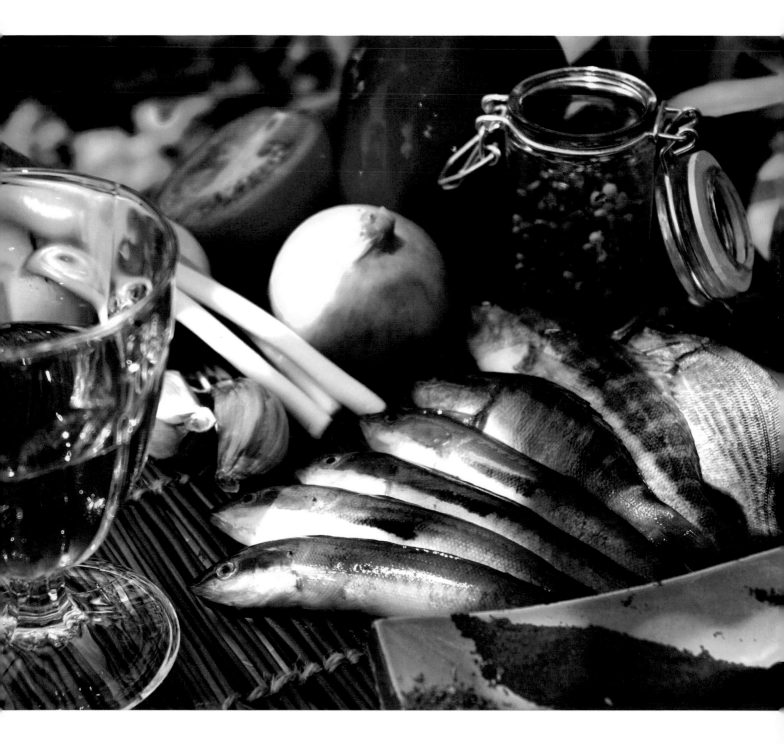

FISH SOUP

Soupe Poissons

FOR THE SOUP:

2½ pounds (1.13 kg) whole small fish

3 tablespoons (45 mL) extra virgin olive oil

1 medium onion, chopped

½ fennel bulb with greens, chopped

1 fresh bay leaf

4 small ripe tomatoes, chopped

3 garlic cloves, minced

Pinch saffron threads

Sea salt and freshly ground black pepper, to taste

2 tablespoons pastis

FOR THE SAUCE:

3 cloves garlic

½ teaspoon sea salt

½ cup extra virgin olive oil

Pinch saffron threads

FOR SERVING:

½ cup (50 g) grated hard cheese

16–20 slices crusty bread, toasted

The best fish soup uses fish you've caught yourself. Of course, sometimes after a fishing trip, you still have to stop by the fish counter. If this happens when you're preparing this recipe, choose only small fish—the more colorful, the better. The fish must be fresh, so make sure their eyes are clear. If you find any small crabs, grab those too, as they will add flavor to the soup. A piece of conger eel would be great for depth of flavor. But whatever you choose, remember that when you get home, you can't tell anyone about stopping by the fish counter.

The best companion for the flavors of this soup is rosé. The pronounced flavors of this dish marry particularly well with a fuller-bodied, lively, and dry rosé.

TO PREPARE THE SOUP:

1. Rinse the fish under cold water. Set aside.

2. In a large stockpot, warm the oil over medium heat. Add the onion, fennel, and bay leaf and cook for 5 to 7 minutes, until the vegetables start to soften. Add the fish, tomatoes, and garlic and continue cooking for 1 to 2 minutes.

3. Raise the heat to medium-high. Add enough water to cover the ingredients (about 3½ to 4 quarts [3.3 to 3.8 L]), bring to a boil, and cook for 10 to 12 minutes. Add the saffron, reduce the heat to medium-low, cover, and cook for 40 minutes. Remove from the heat and set aside to cool.

4. When the soup is cool enough to handle, strain it into a large bowl. Discard the shells, bones, and vegetables. Season to taste with the salt and black pepper. Add the pastis and stir well.

TO PREPARE THE SAUCE:

1. Using a mortar and pestle, crush together the garlic and salt. Slowly whisk in the oil, creating an emulsion. Midway through, add the saffron.

TO SERVE:

1. Serve the soup, topped with the grated cheese, in bowls alongside the bread slathered with sauce.

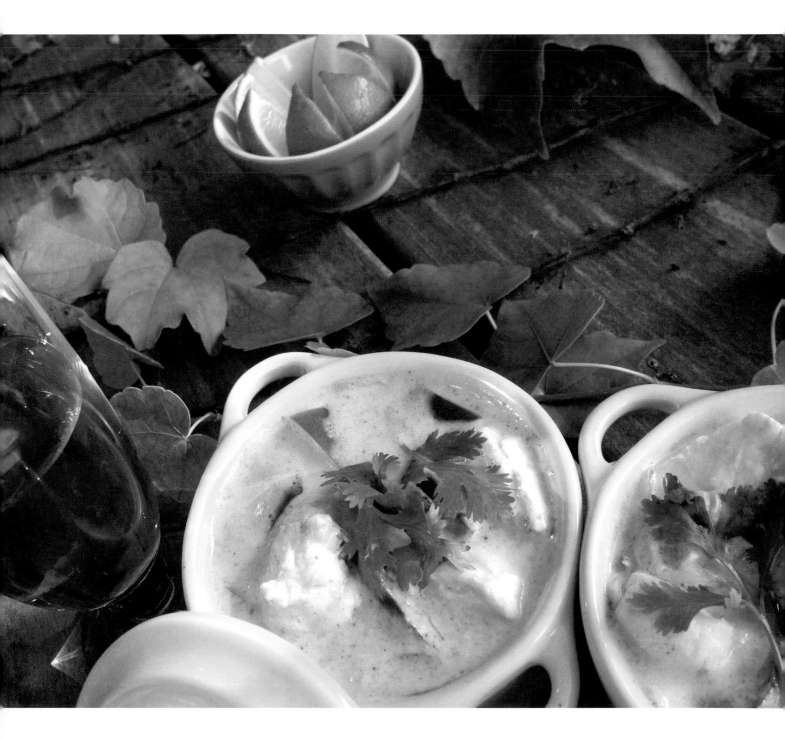

MONKFISH WITH LEMONGRASS AND COCONUT MILK

Lotte à la Citronnelle et au Lait de Coco

2 cups (474 mL) coconut milk

3 tablespoons (3 g) chopped fresh cilantro

4 stalks fresh whole lemongrass

½ teaspoon grated fresh ginger

Juice and zest of 1 lime

Sea salt and freshly ground black pepper, to taste

2 pounds (908 g) monkfish, cut into 4 pieces

3 tablespoons (45 mL) extra virgin olive oil

2 medium onions, chopped

1 green pepper, diced

1 red pepper, diced

4 tomatoes, peeled and diced

Red pepper flakes, to taste (optional)

This recipe depends on the freshness of the fish, so make friends with the fishmonger and request the best monkfish. Sprinkle with cilantro and serve with white rice and a tomato and avocado salad—and a dry, aromatic rosé!

1. In a shallow glass dish, combine the coconut milk, cilantro, lemongrass, ginger, lime juice and zest, a pinch of the salt, and a grind of the black pepper. Add the fish and refrigerate for 4 to 6 hours.

2. In a large sauté pan, warm the oil over medium heat. Add the onions and peppers and cook for 5 to 6 minutes. Add the tomatoes and cook for another 3 to 4 minutes, until the liquid evaporates.

3. Reduce the heat to low. Add the fish and its marinade and cook for 10 to 15 minutes. Remove from the heat.

4. Adjust the salt and black pepper to taste. Add the red pepper flakes, if using. Serve warm.

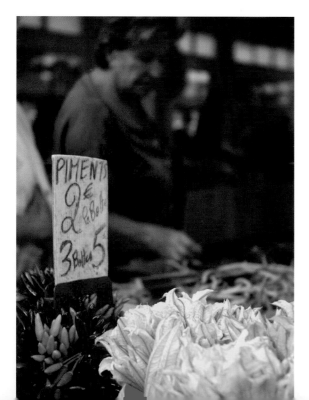

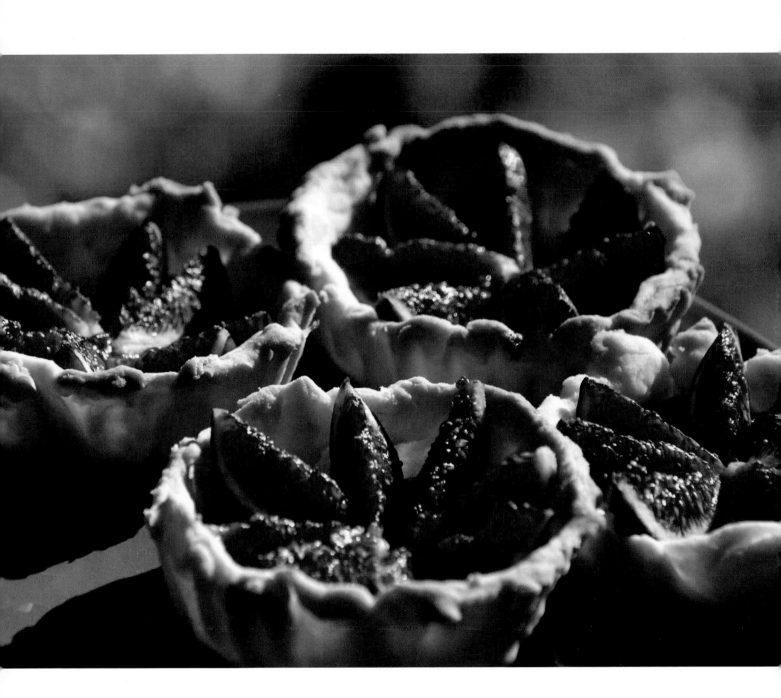

FIG TART

Tarte aux Figues

FOR THE CRUST:

1¼ cups (156 g) all-purpose flour

1 teaspoon granulated sugar

½ teaspoon sea salt

1 stick (8 tablespoons [46 g]) chilled butter, cubed

¼ cup (59 mL) ice water

FOR THE FILLING:

⅓ cup (40 g) confectioners' sugar

1 tablespoon water

Zest of 1 lemon (about 1 tablespoon)

1 pound (454 g) ripe black figs, quartered

2 tablespoons Armagnac or other brandy (optional)

When figs are in season, nothing wakes up the taste buds like the smell of this rich and buttery tart in the oven. The fig, a quintessential Mediterranean fruit, pairs perfectly with round, soft, fruity red wines.

TO PREPARE THE CRUST:

1. In the bowl of a food processor, combine the flour, sugar, and salt. Add the butter and pulse for 15 seconds, until the dough resembles a coarse meal.

2. Slowly add the water, continuing to pulse for another 15 seconds, until clumps start to form. Do not overprocess. The dough should not be a solid ball.

3. Transfer the dough to a very lightly floured work surface and gently form into a ball. Divide in two, and flatten each half into a disc. Wrap the discs in plastic wrap and refrigerate at least 40 minutes. At this point, the dough can be frozen for up to a month.

4. Preheat the oven to 400°F (200°C).

5. Remove 1 disc of the dough from the refrigerator and set aside at room temperature until it starts to soften and can be rolled out. The dough should not be too soft, as it will stick.

6. Between 2 sheets of plastic wrap or wax paper, roll out the dough to a ¼-inch (6-mm) thickness.

7. Transfer the dough to a 9-inch (22.5-cm) tart pan with a removable bottom, and press into the bottom and the flutes of the tart pan. Trim off any excess dough.

TO PREPARE THE FILLING:

1. In a small mixing bowl, combine the powdered sugar, water, and lemon zest and mix well. Brush the inside of the empty tart crust with ½ of the mixture.

2. Layer the fig quarters, cut-sides up, in concentric circles, covering the entire surface of the tart crust.

3. Brush the figs with the remaining sugar mixture. Drizzle with the Armagnac, if using.

4. Bake for 45 minutes. Remove from the oven.

5. Carefully remove the tart from the pan. Serve warm or at room temperature.

SAINT-TROPEZ CUSTARD CAKES

Tartes Tropéziennes

FOR THE BRIOCHES:

1 (¼-ounce [7-g]) packet quick-rise yeast

½ cup (119 mL) warm water (105–110°F [40–43°C])

⅓ cup (64 g) plus 1 teaspoon granulated sugar, divided

2 cups (250 g) all-purpose flour, plus more for folding and cutting

2¼ cups (245 g) cake flour

1½ teaspoons sea salt

6 eggs, room temperature

2½ sticks (283 g) butter, room temperature, cubed, plus more for greasing

2 egg yolks, beaten

FOR THE CHANTILLY:

2 cups (474 mL) milk

1 vanilla bean, cut open

5 egg yolks

½ cup (96 g) granulated sugar

2 tablespoons cornstarch

1 cup (237 mL) whipping cream

FOR ASSEMBLING:

Confectioners' sugar, for dusting

This signature dessert of the seaside town of Saint-Tropez is shrouded in mystery. Ask anyone and they will tell you that the recipe is a secret. So, if you want to keep the secret, don't give this recipe to any of your friends.

When he disembarked in Provence with the Americans in 1945, the enterprising Alexandre Micka opened a bakery in the city hall square of Saint-Tropez. Side by side with pizza, croissants, and pastries, he sold a custard cake whose recipe originated in his native Poland.

Around 10 years later, director Roger Vadim and actors Brigitte Bardot, Curd Jürgens, and a young Jean-Louis Trintignant arrived to film …*And God Created Woman,* a movie that would set the planet on fire upon its release. Micka quickly started supplying them with his creations, and his custard cake became in high demand. "You need to name your dessert," said Bardot to him one day. "Why don't you call it *la tarte de Saint-Tropez?*" Finally, Micka took her advice, but shortened the name to *tarte tropézienne.*

By 1975, *tarte tropézienne* was still just a local favorite. It was then that Jean-Baptiste Doumeng, nick-named Red Billionaire, got Micka to agree to develop a recipe for a frozen *tarte tropézienne* to distribute across Europe. He launched a massive promotional campaign, and *voilà: tarte tropézienne* became an instant success!

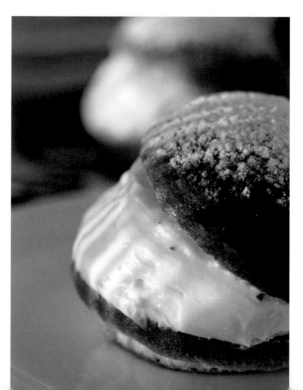

TO PREPARE THE BRIOCHES:

1. In a small mixing bowl, dissolve the yeast in the water. Add 1 teaspoon of the sugar and set aside for 10 minutes.

2. In the bowl of a stand mixer fitted with the dough hook attachment, combine the flours, the remaining ⅓ cup (64 g) of the sugar, and the salt. Add the eggs and mix on low speed for 2 minutes, until the eggs are incorporated. Add the yeast mixture and continue mixing on low speed for another 5 to 6 minutes. Add ½ of the butter cubes and mix until they are incorporated. Add the rest of the butter and continue mixing for 10 minutes, periodically scraping down the side of the bowl.

3. Transfer the dough to a large bowl dusted with flour, cover, and let rise in a warm place for 3 hours, until it has doubled in size.

4. Turn out the dough on a lightly floured work surface. Gently fold it over several times, working out any air bubbles. Return the dough to the bowl, cover with plastic wrap, and refrigerate overnight.

5. Preheat the oven to 350°F (180°C).

6. Remove the dough from the refrigerator and let it warm to room temperature.

7. Generously grease 2 9-inch (22.5-cm) cake pans or 2 muffin pans with butter.

8. Turn out the dough on a lightly floured work surface. Cut it to the measurements of the pans you are using. Place in the pans and let rise in a warm place, uncovered, for 1 hour.

9. Brush the dough with the egg yolks and bake for 45 to 50 minutes, until well browned on top. Remove from the oven.

10. Remove the brioches from the pans and set aside to cool on a wire rack.

TO PREPARE THE CHANTILLY:

1. In a medium saucepan, combine the milk and vanilla over medium heat. Bring to a boil. Remove from the heat.

2. In a medium mixing bowl, beat together the egg yolks and sugar until the mixture is thick and pale. Add the cornstarch and slowly temper in the milk–vanilla mixture, 1 cup (237 mL) at a time, making sure not to scramble the eggs.

3. Return the mixture to the saucepan and cook over low heat, stirring constantly, until the pastry cream comes to a boil and thickens. Remove from the heat.

4. Transfer the pastry cream to a bowl and cover with plastic wrap (make sure the wrap touches the surface of the pastry cream, in order to prevent a crust from forming). Set aside to cool to room temperature.

5. In a very cold bowl, whip the whipping cream. Add the whipped cream to the pastry cream and stir well, creating a Chantilly.

TO ASSEMBLE THE CAKES:

1. Halve each brioche and fill with the Chantilly. Dust with the confectioners' sugar and serve immediately.

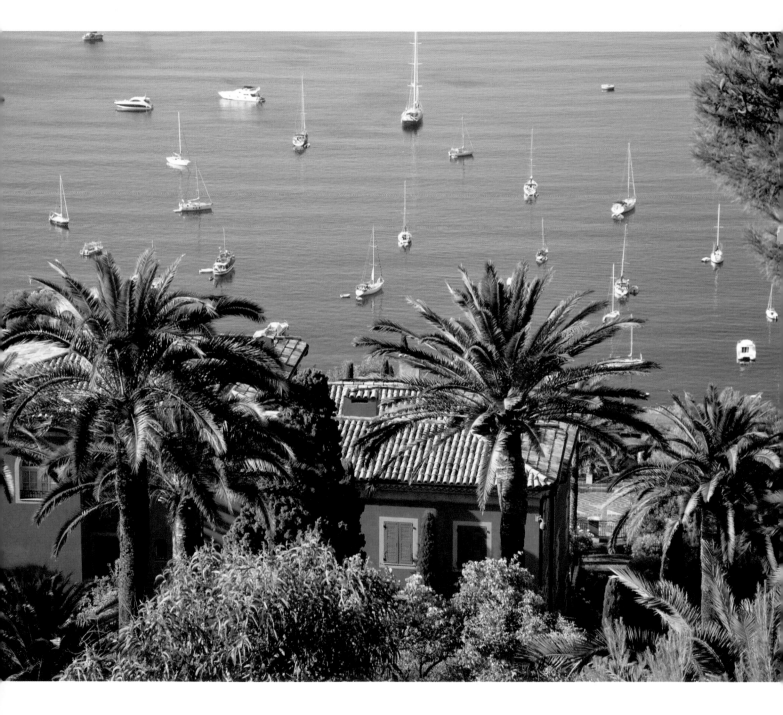

Nice and the Riviera

NICE, THE LUMINOUS CAPITAL OF THE FRENCH RIVIERA, IS A great food city. It is one of only two cities in France recognized as having its own cuisine (the other is Lyon). Niçoise cuisine is a combination of the flavorful produce that grows around the city and many external influences; Italy, for example, is a step away, so the Italian influence is obvious in Nice's many pasta and gnocchi dishes.

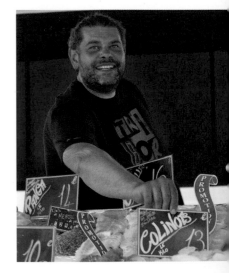

Nice's unique and delectable food begins with such locally grown items as zucchini and zucchini flowers, mesclun, tomatoes, and Swiss chard. Chefs and home cooks alike revere the zucchini flower, competing for who will have the tastiest, lightest, most ethereal zucchini-flower *beignet*. And local tomatoes, eggplant, zucchini, and onions become vessels for the many different fillings that make *petits farcis*, or small, stuffed vegetables, one of the signature dishes of Nice. Stuffed vegetables are common in Provence, but in Nice those vegetables are small, possibly because they are part of the repertoire of street foods you can eat with your hands—another thing Nice is famous for.

This is a town where people are outside at all times enjoying the warm weather, and as such, Nice is home to a number of unique street foods: *socca*, a thick chickpea-flour pancake; *pan bagnat*, a crusty roll stuffed with *salade Niçoise*; sardine *beignets*; *pissaladière*, a pizza-like dish covered with caramelized

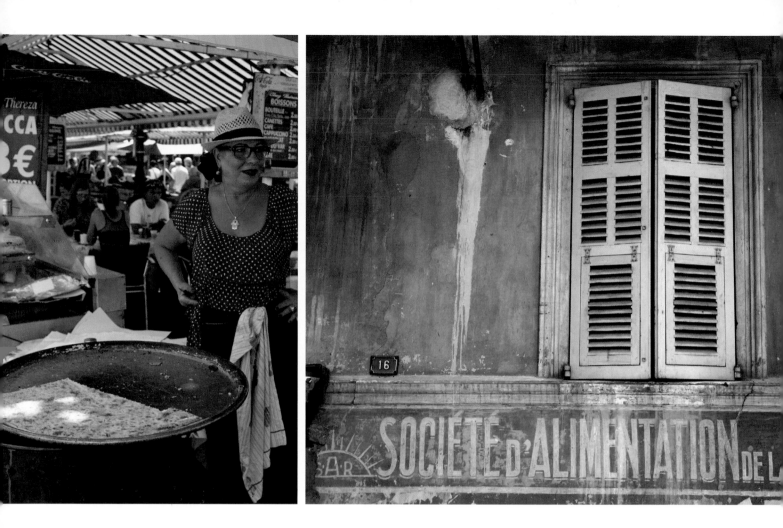

onions, olives, and anchovies; and, of course, *petits farcis*. All of these finger foods pair perfectly with a glass of chilled rosé.

Nice's numerous markets offer fresh local products, often sold by the very people who make them. Strolling the Cours Saleya, or the less touristy (but no less appealing) Marché de la Libération, you can feast your eyes on fresh fruits and vegetables, flowers in brilliant colors, local nougat, *pâte de fruit*, and olive oil.

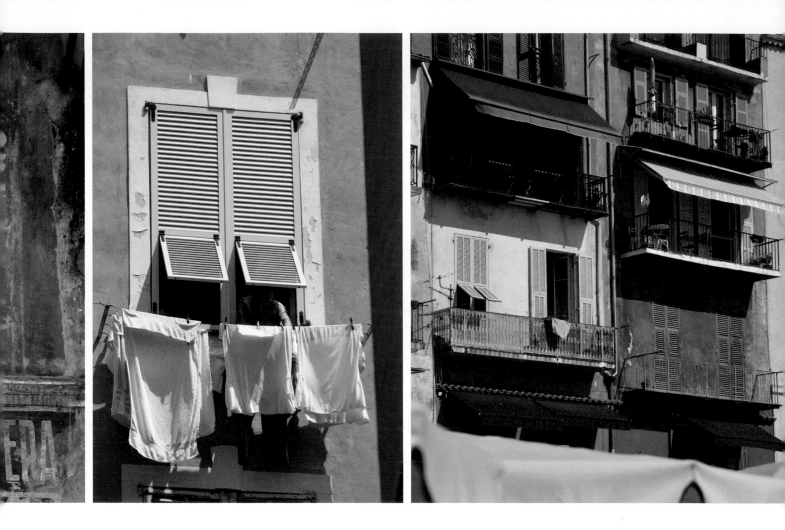

As it's located on the Mediterranean, Nice of course has delicious seafood. Sardines are one of the signature dishes of Nice, but unlike in Marseille, where they are simply grilled or baked and drizzled with lemon, here they are stuffed with Swiss chard and baked—a true Niçois delicacy!

Here, food is a lifestyle. So, whether you eat in one of the many restaurants, or simply grab some street food and enjoy life outdoors, you are tasting *l'art de vivre*.

FOUGASSE WITH TOMATOES, OLIVES, AND PEPPERS

————————————————— YIELD: 6 SERVINGS —————————————————

FOR THE DOUGH:

1 packet instant dry yeast dissolved in 1 cup (237 mL) lukewarm water

1 teaspoon granulated sugar

2 cups (250 g) all-purpose flour, plus more for kneading

½ teaspoon sea salt

3 tablespoons (45 mL) extra virgin olive oil, plus more for greasing

FOR THE FILLING:

5 tablespoons (75 mL) extra virgin olive oil, divided

2 red bell peppers, cored and cut into strips

2 yellow bell peppers, cored and cut into strips

2 green bell peppers, cored and cut into strips

½ teaspoon sea salt, plus more to taste

2 medium onions, chopped

2 medium tomatoes, seeded and chopped

1 cup (144 g) green or black olives, pitted and chopped

1 teaspoon minced fresh thyme

1 teaspoon minced fresh savory

½ teaspoon minced fresh rosemary

This *fougasse*, a Provençal bread stuffed with vegetables, is rich and savory, almost a meal in and of itself. Pair with a structured-but-dry rosé for a perfect appetizer.

TO PREPARE THE DOUGH:

1. Add the sugar to the yeast mixture, stir, and set aside for 5 to 7 minutes, until the yeast starts to bubble.

2. In a large mixing bowl, combine the flour and salt. When the yeast is bubbling, add it to the flour mixture and stir. Add 3 tablespoons (45 mL) of the oil and mix well to combine. If the dough is too wet, add more flour. The dough should not be sticky.

3. Turn out the dough on a lightly floured work surface. Knead for 8 to 10 minutes, until smooth. Form the dough into a ball.

4. Lightly grease a large bowl with the oil. Place the dough ball into the prepared bowl. Cover with a damp kitchen towel and let rise in a warm, draft-free place for 1 to 1½ hours, until the dough has doubled in size.

TO PREPARE THE FILLING:

1. In a medium sauté pan, warm 2 tablespoons of the oil over medium heat. Add the peppers and a sprinkling of salt and cook for 5 to 7 minutes, until the peppers soften. Remove from the heat and set aside.

2. In another medium sauté pan, warm the remaining 3 tablespoons (45 mL) of oil over medium heat. Add the onions and ½ teaspoon of the salt and cook for 8 to 10 minutes, until the onions are translucent. Remove from the heat and set aside.

3. Preheat the oven to 400°F (200°C).

4. Lightly oil a large baking sheet.

5. Punch down the dough and cut it in half. Pat each half into an oval that's about ¼ inch (6 mm) thick.

6. Transfer 1 oval to the prepared baking sheet. Layer with the tomatoes, onions, and olives. Cover with the second dough oval and press the edges to close the *fougasse*. Score the top diagonally.

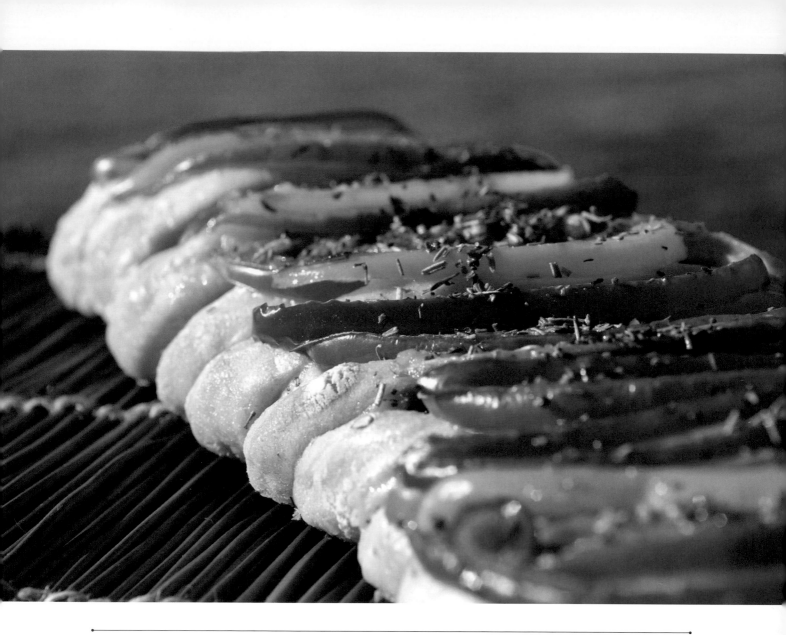

7. Layer the peppers on top, alternating the three colors for visual appeal. Sprinkle with the minced herbs and season to taste with sea salt.

8. Bake for 40 to 45 minutes, until the *fougasse* is golden. Remove from the oven and let cool to room temperature before serving.

ONION TART

Pissaladière

FOR THE DOUGH:

1 packet instant dry yeast dissolved in 1 cup (237 mL) lukewarm water

1 teaspoon granulated sugar

2 cups (250 g) all-purpose flour, plus more for kneading

½ teaspoon sea salt

3 tablespoons (45 mL) extra virgin olive oil, plus more for greasing

FOR THE TOPPING:

5 tablespoons (75 mL) extra virgin olive oil

3 pounds (1.3 kg) yellow onions, thinly sliced (about 4 large onions)

6 cloves garlic, minced

2 teaspoons granulated sugar

1 teaspoon minced fresh thyme

½ teaspoon minced fresh rosemary

½ teaspoon minced fresh savory

½ teaspoon sea salt

Freshly ground black pepper, to taste

½ cup (72 g) black Niçoise olives, pitted

4–6 anchovy fillets, packed in oil

A popular Niçois street food, *pissaladière* was named after the salted fish paste *(lou pissala)* that was used as a topping long ago, when whole anchovies were too expensive. After the anchovies were filleted and preserved in salt or oil, the leftovers (that is, the guts and bones) were combined with salt and used as a topping for *pissaladière*. Today, anchovy fillets are used, but many Provençals remember their grandparents making *pissala*, as well as the ensuing aromas.

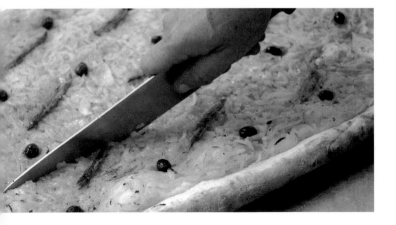

TO PREPARE THE DOUGH:

1. In a mixing bowl, add the sugar to the yeast mixture. Stir and set aside for 5 to 7 minutes, until the yeast starts to bubble.

2. In a large mixing bowl, combine the flour and salt. When the yeast is bubbling, add it to the flour mixture and stir. Add 3 tablespoons (45 mL) of the oil and mix well to combine. If the dough is too wet, add more flour. The dough should not be sticky.

3. Turn out the dough on a lightly floured work surface. Knead for 8 to 10 minutes, until smooth. Form the dough into a ball.

4. Lightly grease a large bowl with the oil. Place the dough ball into the prepared bowl, cover with a damp kitchen towel, and let rise in a warm, draft-free place for 1 to 1½ hours, until the dough has doubled in size.

5. Grease a large baking sheet with the oil. Using your hands, flatten the dough onto the sheet. Make sure the dough is evenly distributed. Let rise for another 30 minutes.

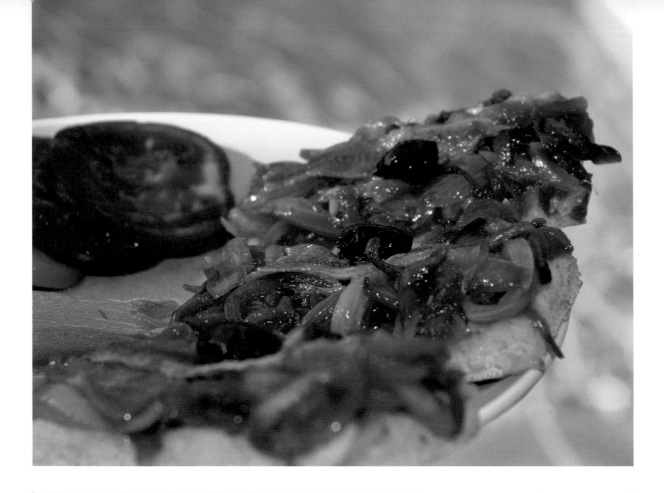

TO PREPARE THE TOPPING:

1. In a large sauté pan, warm the oil over medium-high heat. Add the onions and cook for 7 to 9 minutes. Add the garlic, stir well, and cook for another minute. Add the sugar, stir well, and cook for 5 to 7 minutes. Add the herbs, ½ teaspoon of the salt, and a grind of black pepper and continue cooking for another 20 minutes or so, until the onions start to turn brown.

2. Preheat the oven to 325°F (160°C).

3. Bake the dough for 25 minutes. Remove from the oven and cover with an even layer of the cooked onion mixture.

4. Raise the oven temperature to 375°F (190°C). Bake for another 25 to 30 minutes. Remove from the oven and distribute the anchovies and olives on top of the tart.

5. Serve warm or at room temperature. The tart will keep in the refrigerator for up to 2 days. If refrigerated, reheat in the oven at 375°F (190°C) for 15 minutes before serving.

NIÇOISE SALAD

Salade Niçoise

1 clove garlic, halved

4 cups (960 g) mesclun

6 small tomatoes, sliced

½ cucumber, sliced (optional)

2 celery ribs, thinly sliced

8 radishes, thinly sliced

2 small, sweet cubanelle peppers, sliced

3 green onions, sliced

1½ cups (225 g) fresh shelled fava beans

3 hard-boiled eggs, sliced

6 salt-packed anchovies, rinsed well and chopped

¾ cup (108 g) black Niçoise olives

Sea salt and freshly ground black pepper, to taste

8 fresh basil leaves, for garnish

Extra virgin olive oil, for drizzling

Salade Niçoise is a specialty of Nice that has spread around the world in many different variations. It is a delicious combination of fresh seasonal vegetables, hard-boiled eggs, and fish, finished with a good extra virgin olive oil and black Niçoise olives. *Salade Niçoise* is a popular appetizer on Provençal menus, but it can also be a full meal. The original recipe featured tomatoes, salted three times; in modern times, fresh tomatoes are used. In the past, tuna was expensive and only used for holiday meals; anchovies were more common. Traditional *Salade Niçoise* does not include cooked vegetables or rice.

Of course, the perfect accompaniment for this traditional Provençal dish is a dry, aromatic, and perfectly chilled rosé.

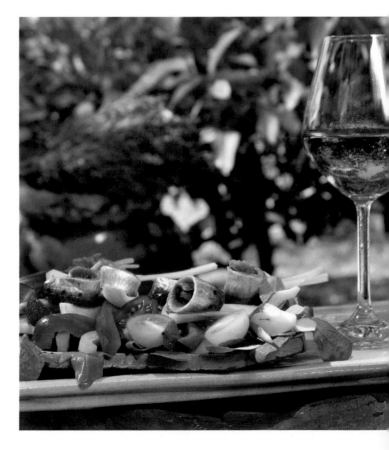

1. Lightly rub 4 salad plates with the garlic. Discard the garlic.

2. Divide the mesclun among the plates and layer with the tomatoes, cucumber (if using), celery, radishes, peppers, green onions, and fava beans. Finish with the hard-boiled eggs, anchovies, and olives. Season to taste with the salt and black pepper.

3. Garnish each plate with 2 basil leaves. Drizzle some of the oil over each plate. Serve immediately.

MINI STUFFED VEGETABLES

Mini Légumes Farcis

8 small tomatoes

2 tablespoons extra virgin olive oil, plus more for drizzling

1 small onion, chopped

2 cloves garlic, minced

½ pound (227 g) ground beef

¼ pound (114 g) sausage (1 sausage), casing removed

Sea salt and freshly ground black pepper, to taste

1 egg

2 tablespoons minced fresh parsley

2 tablespoons minced fresh basil

2 medium zucchini, sliced lengthwise into ⅛-inch (3-mm) slices

2 small Japanese eggplants, sliced lengthwise into ⅛-inch (3-mm) slices

2 red bell peppers, grilled, peeled, and seeded

This iconic Niçois dish is often served as a street food. Stands sell *petits farcis* all day, and you can grab one on the go or take a seat and enjoy it with a glass of chilled rosé—preferably one that is fuller bodied and flavorful.

1. Remove the tops from the tomatoes and reserve them. Remove and discard the tomatoes' seeds, but reserve their juice. Set aside.

2. Preheat the oven to 375°F (190°C).

3. In a medium sauté pan, warm the oil over medium heat. Add the onion and cook for 5 minutes, until it starts to soften. Add the garlic and continue cooking for 1 minute.

4. Add the beef and sausage to the sauté pan. Break it up and stir well. Add ½ teaspoon of the salt and a grind of black pepper. Continue cooking for 5 to 6 minutes, until the meat has browned. Add the reserved tomato juice and continue cooking until the juice has reduced by about ⅓. Remove from the heat.

5. Transfer to a bowl. Set aside to cool slightly. Season to taste with the salt and black pepper. Add the egg, parsley, and basil and stir well.

6. Using a tablespoon measure, fill the tomatoes with the mixture and cover with the reserved tomato tops. Form the eggplant, zucchini, and peppers into little cones (see photo) and fill them with the mixture as well.

7. Place the stuffed vegetables into a medium baking dish, drizzle with a little bit of the oil, and bake for 40 to 45 minutes, until the vegetables are cooked through. Remove from the oven.

8. Serve warm or at room temperature.

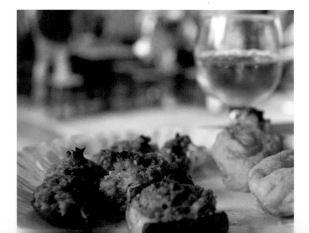

SWISS CHARD TART WITH GRILLED FOIE GRAS AND WILD MUSHROOMS

Tourte de Blettes, Escalope de Foie Gras Grillée, et Champignons Sauvages

━━━━━━━━━━ **YIELD: 4 SERVINGS** ━━━━━━━━━━

I package puff pastry, defrosted

I egg yolk, beaten

4 ½-inch (13-mm) slices foie gras

4 tablespoons (59 mL) extra virgin olive oil, divided

I ½ pounds (681 g) wild mushrooms (chanterelles, morels, or other wild variety), cleaned and chopped

Sea salt and freshly ground black pepper, to taste

I tablespoon butter

I leek, chopped

I bunch Swiss chard, stems removed and green parts chopped

2 tablespoons chopped fresh parsley

2 teaspoons chopped fresh chives

10 fresh mint leaves

4 dried figs, chopped

4 dried apricots, chopped

3 tablespoons (42 g) raisins, soaked in warm water for 5 minutes and then drained

2 tablespoons pine nuts

4 tablespoons (56 g) crème fraîche

3 tablespoons (27 g) sliced almonds, toasted

The Auberge de la Madone is a hotel in the mountain village of Peillon. Christian and Thomas Millo, the father-and-son team who runs the hotel, delight their guests with dishes that combine the robust flavors of inland Provence and the sophistication of modern cuisine. For a perfect start to a refined dinner party, pair this tart with a well-structured rosé.

1. Cut out 4 3-inch (7.5-cm) circles from the puff pastry. Brush the circles with the egg yolk. Place them on a nonstick baking sheet and bake according to the package instructions. Remove from the oven and set aside. (The puff pastry can be prepared ahead of time and reheated before serving.)

2. Preheat a grill or stovetop griddle. Grill the foie gras for 3 to 4 minutes on each side. Remove from the heat. Set aside.

3. In a large sauté pan, warm 2 tablespoons of the oil over medium-high heat. Add the mushrooms and cook for 6 to 8 minutes, until soft. Sprinkle with the salt and set aside.

4. In the same sauté pan, warm the remaining 2 tablespoons of oil and the butter over medium heat. Add the leek, Swiss chard, and a pinch of salt and cook for 8 to 10 minutes, until the greens are wilted. Add the herbs, stir well, and cook for 3 minutes. Add the figs, apricots, raisins, and pine nuts, stir well, and cook for 2 minutes. Season to taste with the salt and black pepper. Remove from the heat. Add the crème fraîche and stir well. Set aside.

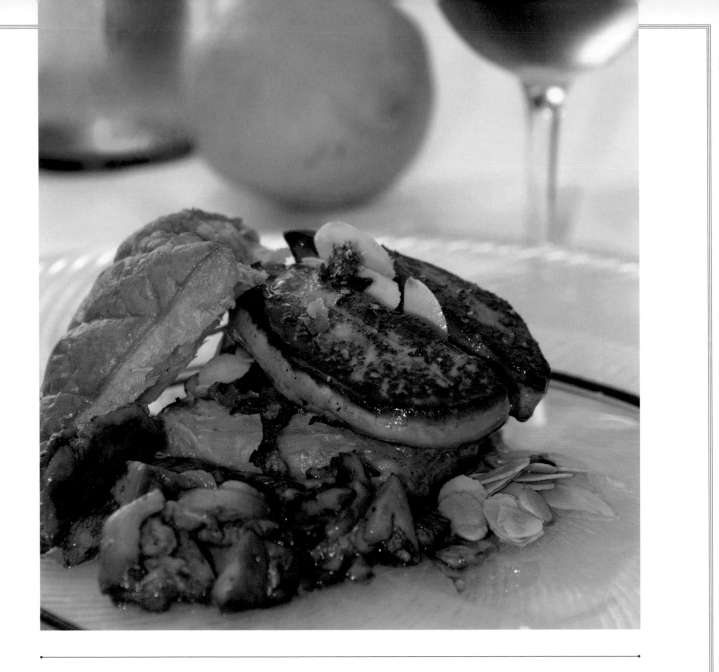

5. Halve the puff pastry circles lengthwise and place 1 half on each of 4 serving plates. Top with the cooked greens and a slice of foie gras. Cover with the other puff pastry half. Sprinkle with the almonds. Divide the mushrooms among the 4 plates. Serve warm.

STUFFED SARDINES

Sardines Farcies à la Niçoise

12 small sardines, cleaned, heads removed

2 tablespoons butter

1 bunch spinach, washed

3½ ounces (99 g) mild chèvre (½ cup)

⅓ cup (45 g) pine nuts

1 egg

2 tablespoons chopped fresh parsley

Sea salt and freshly ground black pepper, to taste

2 tablespoons extra virgin olive oil, for brushing

2 lemons, sliced, for serving

Sardines stuffed with greens are a specialty of Nice and pair well with a mesclun salad or boiled potatoes. Serve this dish with a more robust rosé that can match the depth of flavor of the sardines.

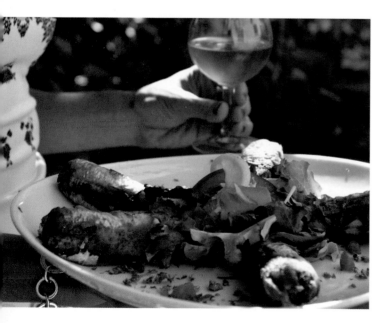

1. Slice open the sardines lengthwise, so they will lie flat on a work surface. Do not separate the fillets. Rinse in cold water and set aside.

2. In a medium sauté pan, warm the butter over medium heat. Add the spinach and cook for 2 to 3 minutes, until it has wilted. Remove from the heat.

3. Drain the spinach. Once it has cooled enough to be handled, finely chop it.

4. Preheat the oven to 375°F (190°C).

5. In a mixing bowl, combine the spinach, chèvre, pine nuts, egg, and parsley. Season with the salt and a grind of the black pepper and stir to combine.

6. Line a baking sheet with aluminum foil and lightly brush with some of the oil. Layer the sardines, skin-side down, on the foil. Place 1 heaping tablespoon of the spinach mixture on half of each sardine. Cover with the other half, pressing lightly to close the sardines. Brush the tops with the oil and bake for 15 minutes. Remove from the oven.

7. Serve warm with the lemon slices.

GNOCCHI

2 pounds (908 g) potatoes
(about 6 medium potatoes)

¾ cup (143 g) coarse sea salt,
plus more to taste

¾ cup (124 g) soft wheat flour with a
low protein content, such as Wondra,
plus more for rolling

2 small or 1 large shallot, minced
(about ½ cup)

1 egg

1 egg yolk

3 tablespoons (43 g) fromage blanc*

1 gallon (3.8 L) water

1 tablespoon salt

Extra virgin olive oil, for brushing

Sea salt and freshly ground black
pepper, to taste

Potato gnocchi, though Italian in origin, is common in Nice. The most important step in making great gnocchi is the choice of potatoes. For best results, choose starchy potatoes, such as russet or Yukon gold; Yukon gold has the advantage of a richer, nutty flavor.

In this recipe, the potatoes are baked on a bed of coarse sea salt instead of being boiled. That way, they do not absorb water; in fact, the salt draws water out of the potatoes, bringing you even closer to gnocchi perfection.

To avoid sticky gnocchi, make them just before you cook them. You can refrigerate them for several hours on a plate lined with paper towels, but they are best enjoyed when they are very fresh.

These gnocchi are so delicious that they can be served with only a drizzle of extra virgin olive oil and some delicious cheese such as Parmigiano–Reggiano, Gorgonzola, or fresh ricotta. Gnocchi are also excellent with vegetable or meat sauces, fresh herbs, or even just a touch of nutmeg. And the inevitable glass of rosé, of course.

1. Preheat the oven to 375°F (190°C).

2. Pierce each potato in several places. In a 9-inch (22.5-cm) pie dish, place ¾ cup (143 g) of the salt and rest the potatoes on top. Bake for 1 hour. Remove from the oven and set aside to cool.

3. When the potatoes are cool enough to handle, peel them. Using a potato ricer, rice them into a large bowl.

4. To the bowl of potatoes, add the flour, shallots, egg, egg yolk, and fromage blanc, and stir gently with a spatula until the gnocchi dough comes together. If the dough is too sticky, add a little more flour.

5. Divide the dough into quarters. On a lightly floured work surface, roll each quarter into a snakelike shape ½ inch (13 mm) in diameter. Cut the shapes into bite-sized pieces. Toss the pieces lightly in some of the flour and set aside on a plate.

6. In a large stockpot, bring the water and salt to a boil over medium-high heat. Brush a baking sheet with the oil.

7. Add the gnocchi to the boiling water and cook for 1 to 2 minutes. Remove from the heat.

8. With a slotted spoon, remove the gnocchi from the water and place them on the prepared baking sheet.

9. Transfer the gnocchi to a serving bowl. Toss with whatever topping you are using (cheese, sauce, etc.), adjust the seasoning to taste, and serve immediately.

Fromage blanc is a low-fat or fat-free cheese available in the yogurt section of most grocery stores.

COOKS' NOTE: *All-purpose flour is too high in protein to make great gnocchi, but a combination of 2 parts all-purpose flour and 1 part cake flour works well.*

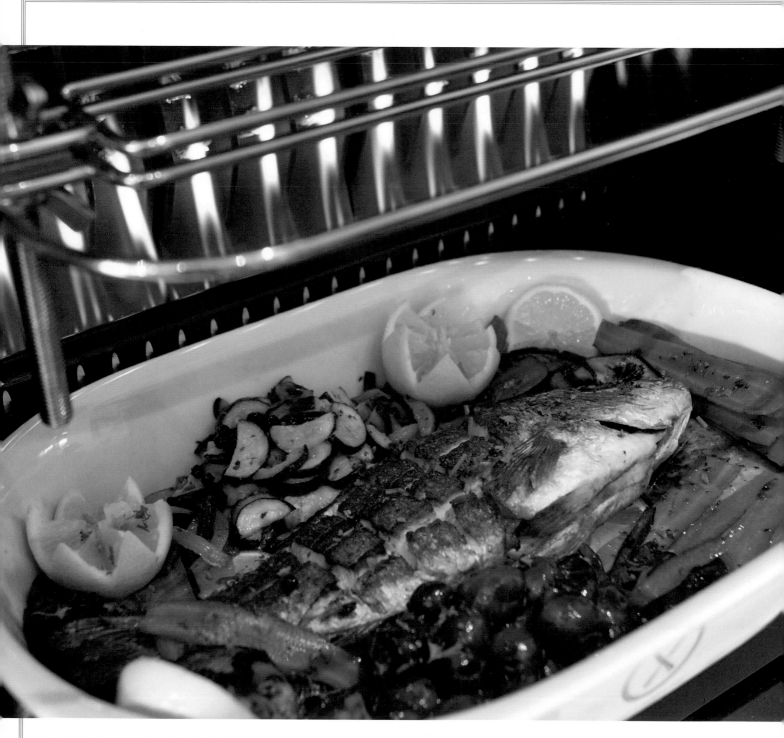

SEA BREAM WITH PASTIS À LA CORNUE

Dourade à La Cornue

YIELD: 4 SERVINGS

1 large sea bream or sea bass, head on (about 2 pounds [908 g])

2 tablespoons extra virgin olive oil

3 tablespoons (45 mL) pastis

Sea salt and freshly ground black pepper, to taste

This surprising recipe from Chef Pasquale Davi (in Cannes) exemplifies this principle of Provençal cooking: fresh ingredients prepared simply give the most delicious results. Serve with plenty of grilled seasonal vegetables and an aromatic, mineral Provence rosé.

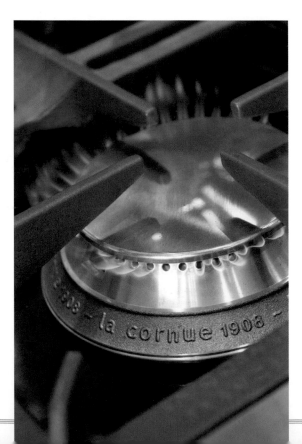

1. Preheat the oven to 375°F (190°C).

2. Pat the fish dry with paper towels, score diagonally, and brush with the oil.

3. Preheat a stovetop griddle or a large cast-iron skillet over medium-high heat.

4. Grill the fish for 3 minutes on each side, until golden brown. Remove from the heat.

5. Place the fish in an ovenproof dish and drizzle with the pastis. Season with salt and black pepper. Bake for 10 minutes, until done but still moist. Remove from the oven.

6. Serve warm.

MEDITERRANEAN COD WITH CARAMELIZED ONIONS AND ANCHOVY–CAPER SAUCE

Fin Colinot de Méditerranée en Pissaladière et Pissalat

— YIELD: 4 SERVINGS —

FOR THE CARAMELIZED ONIONS:

5 tablespoons (75 mL) extra virgin olive oil, divided

1 bunch green onions, white parts cut into 1½-inch (3.8-cm) pieces and thinly sliced lengthwise

½ teaspoon fresh thyme

Sea salt and freshly ground black pepper, to taste

2 medium russet potatoes, peeled, quartered, and thinly sliced

FOR THE ANCHOVY–CAPER SAUCE:

6 anchovy fillets, packed in oil

2 tablespoons extra virgin olive oil

1 tablespoon capers

1 clove garlic

FOR THE VINAIGRETTE:

2 tablespoons tamari sauce

1 tablespoon extra virgin olive oil

1 tablespoon balsamic vinegar

FOR THE FISH:

2 tablespoons extra virgin olive oil

4 cod fillets, skin on

½ tablespoon butter

2 sprigs fresh thyme

2 fresh bay leaves

1 clove garlic, thinly sliced

1 sprig fresh rosemary

Juice of ½ lemon

Sea salt and freshly ground black pepper, to taste

2 tablespoons grated Parmigiano–Reggiano cheese, for sprinkling

¼ cup (36 g) black Niçoise olives, pitted, for garnish

This recipe, by Chef Jacques Chibois of La Bastide Saint-Antoine in Grasse, unmistakably recalls true Mediterranean flavors and combines the authentic ingredients of Provence with a worldly sophistication that elevates the dish to pure elegance. Serve with a dry, mineral rosé.

TO PREPARE THE CARAMELIZED ONIONS:

1. In a large nonstick pan, warm 3 tablespoons (45 mL) of the oil over medium-high heat. Add the onions and cook for 8 to 10 minutes, until they are softened, stirring occasionally. Add the thyme and season with the salt and a grind of the black pepper. Reduce the heat to low and cook for another 15 minutes, until the onions start to turn golden. Transfer to a plate and set aside.

2. Raise the heat to medium-high and warm the remaining oil in the pan. Add the potatoes and cook for 8 to 10 minutes. Season to taste with the salt and black pepper. Add the onions back to the pan, stir well to combine, and cook for 2 minutes. Remove from the heat and set aside.

TO PREPARE THE ANCHOVY–CAPER SAUCE:

1. In a blender or the bowl of a food processor, combine the ingredients. Pulse until the mixture is uniform. Set aside.

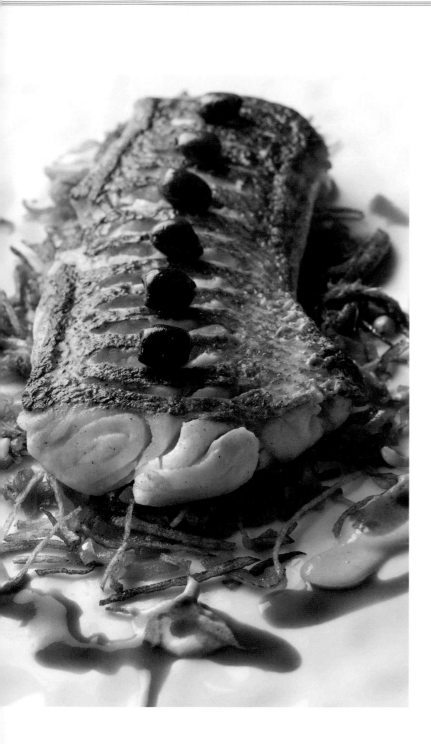

TO PREPARE THE VINAIGRETTE:

1. In a small mixing bowl, combine all ingredients. Whisk until an emulsion forms. Set aside.

TO PREPARE THE FISH:

1. Preheat the oven to 375°F (190°C).

2. In a large nonstick pan, warm the oil over medium-high heat. Add the fish, skin-side down, and cook for 2 minutes. Remove from the heat, transfer to an ovenproof dish, and set aside.

3. Reduce the heat to medium. To the same nonstick pan, add the butter. Once it has melted, add the bay leaves, garlic, rosemary, and thyme. Stir well and cook for 2 minutes.

4. Transfer the herbs and garlic to the ovenproof dish and bake for 5 to 7 minutes, until the fish becomes flaky. Remove from the oven. Remove and discard the herbs and add the lemon juice. Season with the salt and black pepper.

TO PREPARE THE DISH:

1. Divide the onion and potatoes among 4 plates. Sprinkle with the Parmigiano–Reggiano. Place 1 fillet on each plate. Drizzle the vinaigrette around the fish. Drizzle the sauce over the fillets. Garnish with the olives. Serve warm.

TOMATO–SARDINE TARTS

Tartes aux Tomates et aux Sardines

FOR THE GREEN ONION *CONFIT*:

2 tablespoons extra virgin olive oil

4 green onions, chopped

1 clove garlic, minced

1 teaspoon chopped fresh thyme

½ teaspoon chopped fresh rosemary

FOR THE TARTS:

1 package puff pastry

1 tablespoon Dijon mustard

2 small, ripe tomatoes, seeded and sliced into rounds

4 sardine fillets

2 tablespoons pesto, for topping

Sea salt and freshly ground black pepper, to taste

These tarts are as delicious as they are surprising. Pair with a lively Provence rosé for a perfect start to a dinner or even on their own as a light dinner.

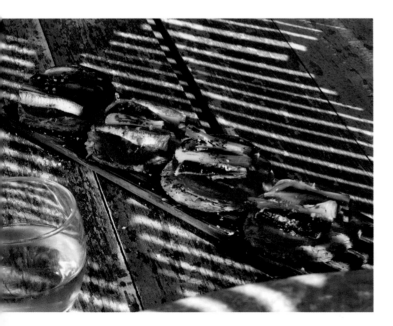

TO PREPARE THE GREEN ONION *CONFIT*:

1. In a medium sauté pan, warm the oil over medium heat. Add the onions and cook for 6 minutes. Reduce the heat to medium-low. Add the garlic, thyme, and rosemary, and continue cooking for 5 to 6 minutes. Remove from the heat and set aside.

TO PREPARE THE TARTS:

1. Bake the puff pastry according to the package instructions. Remove from the oven and set aside to cool to room temperature.

2. Preheat the oven to 400°F (200°C). Line a baking sheet with parchment paper.

3. Cut out 4 circles from the puff pastry sheet. Place the circles on the prepared baking sheet. Brush them with the mustard and top with the tomatoes, sardine fillets, and onion *confit*. Bake for 12 to 14 minutes. Remove from the oven.

4. Top each tart with a dollop of the pesto. Season with salt and black pepper and serve warm.

ZUCCHINI FLOWERS WITH CHÈVRE

Fleurs de Courgettes Farcies

Juice of 1 lemon

4 large or 8 small fresh artichokes

1 cup (237 mL) vegetable stock

½ cup (119 mL) extra virgin olive oil

2 cloves garlic

¼ teaspoon ground coriander seeds

Sea salt and freshly ground black pepper, to taste

6 ounces (170 g) fresh, mild chèvre (⅔ cup)

½ rib celery, finely chopped

8 zucchini flowers

2–3 cups (60–90 g) mesclun

2 tablespoons balsamic vinegar, divided

4 cherry tomatoes, for garnish

Zucchini flowers are among Provence's delicacies. They are best stuffed with a young, mild goat cheese that won't overwhelm the delicate flavor of the flower. Pair with a delicate, dry Provence rosé.

1. Fill a medium bowl with water and add the lemon juice.

2. To clean the artichokes, cut off the top third of each one, including the spiny tops. Remove the outer leaves by peeling them back until they snap. Using a paring knife, peel the stem to remove the fibrous outer layer. Remove any remaining tough, fibrous, dark green parts on the outside of the artichoke heart. With a spoon, scoop out the chokes and clean the inside of the artichoke. Immediately put the artichokes in the bowl of lemon water.

3. Preheat the oven to 400°F (200°C).

4. In a small saucepan, bring the vegetable stock, oil, garlic, coriander, a pinch of salt, and a grind of black pepper to a boil over medium-high heat. Add the artichokes. Reduce the heat to medium and cook for 10 minutes. Drain the artichokes, reserving the cooking liquid. When the artichokes are cool enough to handle, dice them.

5. In a medium mixing bowl, combine the artichokes, chèvre, celery, and 3 to 4 tablespoons (45–59 mL) of the reserved cooking liquid. Stir well.

6. Gently open the zucchini flowers. Using a spoon, fill each flower with as much of the artichoke–chèvre mixture as it can hold.

7. Arrange the flowers in an ovenproof dish. Drizzle with 3 tablespoons (45 mL) of the reserved cooking liquid and bake for 5 to 7 minutes. Remove from the oven, cool to room temperature, and refrigerate for 2 to 4 hours.

8. Place 2 zucchini flowers on each of 4 plates. Add some mesclun, dressing it with a drizzle some of the reserved cooking liquid and ¼ to ½ tablespoon of the balsamic vinegar per plate. Garnish with the tomatoes and serve.

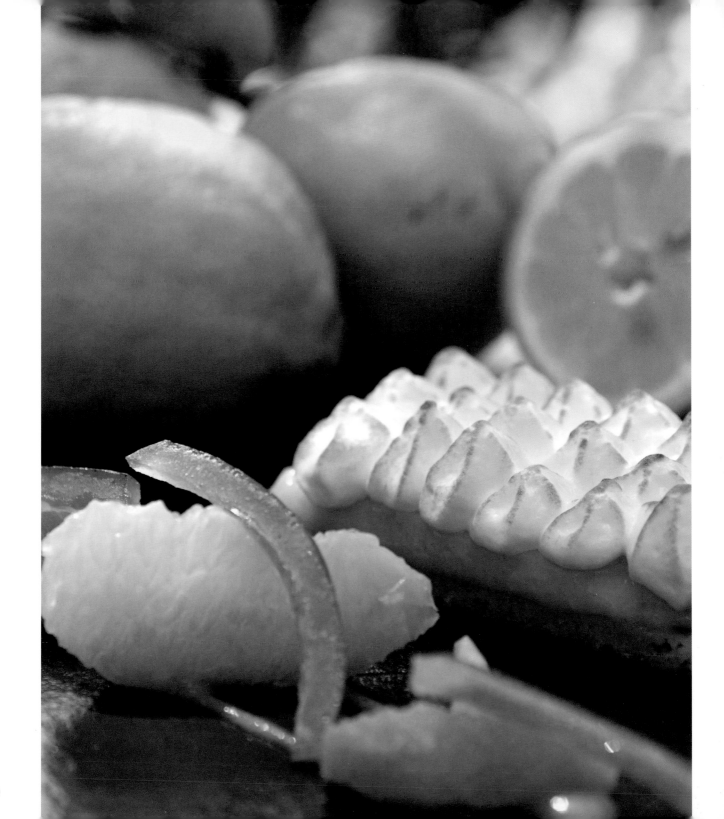

LEMON TART

Tarte au Citron

FOR THE CRUST:

2 cups (250 g) unbleached all-purpose flour, plus more for rolling

7 ounces (199 g) unsalted butter

½ cups (96 g) granulated sugar

¼ teaspoon salt

I egg

I egg yolk

I teaspoon lemon zest

¾ teaspoon pure vanilla extract

FOR THE FILLING:

8 ounces (½ pound [227 g]) crème fraîche

¾ cup (144 g) granulated sugar

3 eggs, lightly beaten

Juice of 4 lemons

4 tablespoons (23 g) butter, softened and cubed

Lemon slices or meringue, for garnish

This delicious and refreshing dessert is the essence of the French Riviera, where the intense sun ripens lemons and infuses them with unrivaled sweetness. Each bite will transport you there. Immerse yourself in sunshine.

TO PREPARE THE CRUST:

1. In a large mixing bowl, combine the flour, butter, sugar, and salt. Mix until crumbly.

2. In a medium mixing bowl, combine the egg, egg yolk, lemon zest, and vanilla extract and beat lightly with a fork. Add the egg mixture to the flour mixture and beat with an electric mixer on low speed for 2 minutes, or until a dough forms.

3. Turn out the dough on a lightly floured work surface. Dust your hands with flour and knead the dough for 1 minute. Wrap the dough in plastic wrap and chill in the refrigerator for at least 1 hour (or up to 4 days). (If you chill the dough for longer than 1 hour, let it warm slightly before rolling it out.)

4. Preheat the oven to 400°F (200°C).

5. On a lightly floured work surface, roll out the dough to a ¼-inch (6-mm) thickness. Transfer the dough to a 9-inch (22.5-cm) tart dish with a removable bottom. Trim off any excess dough. Bake for 25 minutes. Remove from the oven and set aside to cool to room temperature.

TO PREPARE THE FILLING AND ASSEMBLE THE TART:

1. In a mixing bowl, whip the crème fraîche until it is light and airy. Set aside.

2. In a small saucepan, combine the sugar, eggs, and lemon juice over low heat. Stir well. Cook, stirring constantly, for 15 minutes. Remove from the heat.

3. Transfer to a bowl. Add the butter and stir well to incorporate. Set aside to cool to room temperature. Fold in the whipped crème fraîche.

4. Pour the filling into the crust and refrigerate for at least 1 hour, or until ready to serve. Just before serving, garnish with the lemon slices or with meringue that has been browned under a broiler.

Resources

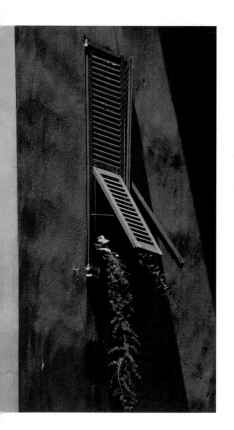

GENERAL

Wines of Provence
www.provencewineusa.com and
www.vinsdeprovence.com

Route des Vins de Provence
www.routedesvinsdeprovence.com

Marseille Regional Tourism Board
www.tourismepaca.fr

**Côte d'Azur Regional
Tourism Bureau**
www.frenchriviera-tourism.com

AIX-EN-PROVENCE AND HAUTE PROVENCE

Bouches du Rhône Tourism Board
www.visitprovence.com

Aix-en-Provence Office of Tourism
www.aixenprovencetourism.com

**Moustiers-Sainte-Marie Office of
Tourism**
www.moustiers.eu/?lang=en

**Coteaux Varois en Provence
Maison des Vins**
www.coteaux-varois.com

Vinothèque Sainte Victoire
www.vins-sainte-victoire.com

L'Occitane
www.loccitane.com

Chocolaterie Puyricard
www.puyricard.fr

**L'Atelier des Chefs
Aix-en-Provence**
www.atelierdeschefs.fr

Confiserie du Roy Rene
www.calisson.com

Fromagerie du Passage
www.lafromageriedupassage.fr

MARSEILLE

Marseille Office of Tourism
www.marseille-tourisme.com

Gourméditerannée
www.mp2013.fr/whats-cooking/
gourmediterranec/?lang=en

La Maison du Pastis
www.lamaisondupastis.com

Le Four des Navettes
www.fourdesnavettes.com

CÔTE VAROISE

Saint-Tropez Office of Tourism
www.ot-saint-tropez.com

Côtes de Provence Maison des Vins
www.maison-des-vins.fr

Association des Vins de La Londe
www.cotesdeprovence-lalonde.com

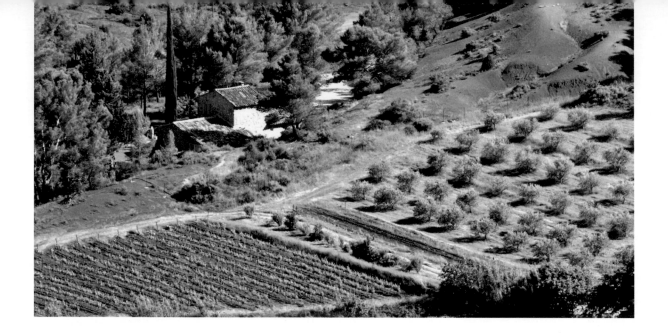

NICE AND THE RIVIERA

Nice Office of Tourism
www.nicetourisme.com

Grasse Office of Tourism
www.grasse.fr

Antibes Office of Tourism
www.antibesjuanlespins.com

Menton Office of Tourism
www.tourisme-menton.fr/
-Menton-French-Riviera-.html

Huilerie Sainte Anne
www.huilerie-sainte-anne.com

Confiserie Florian
www.confiserieflorian.com

Fragonard
www.fragonard.com

La Citronneraie
www.lacitronneraie.com

Maison Barale
www.barale-raviolis.com

La Cornue, Cook, and Toques
www.lacornue.com/qc/distributeurs
/article/4-galerie-la-cornue-cannes

RESTAURANTS

**Bastide Saint Antoine
(Chef Jacques Chibois)**
www.jacques-chibois.com/uk/index.
php

**Hôtel Villa Belrose
(Chef Thierry Thiercelin)**
www.villa-belrose.com

**Hôtel l'Intercontinental, Marseille
(Chef Lionel Levy)**
www.intercontinental.com

**L'Auberge de la Madone (Chefs
Christian and Thomas Millo)**
www.auberge-madone-peillon.com

**Le Phébus
(Chef Xavier Mathieu)**
www.lephebus.com

**The Setai, Miami Beach
(Chef Mathias Gervais)**
www.thesetaihotel.com

l'Escalinada
www.escalinada.fr

L'Ane Rouge
www.anerougenice.com

Oliviera
www.oliviera.com

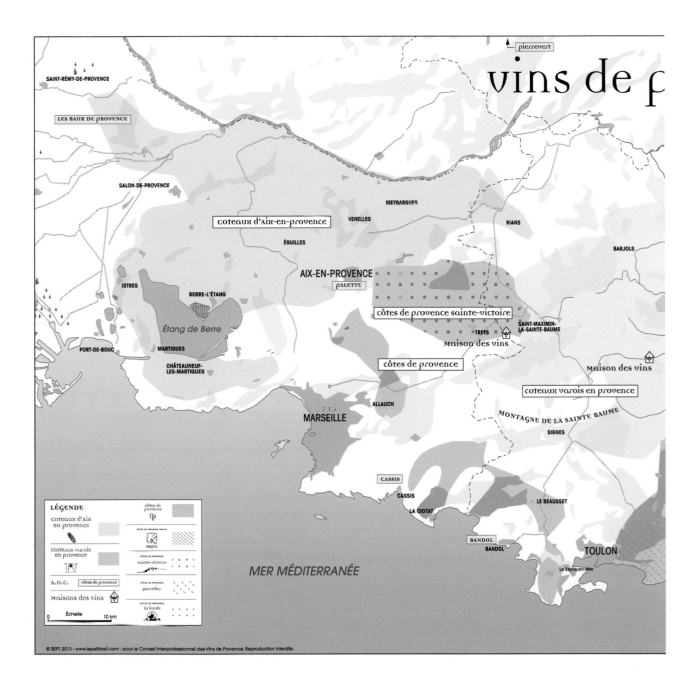

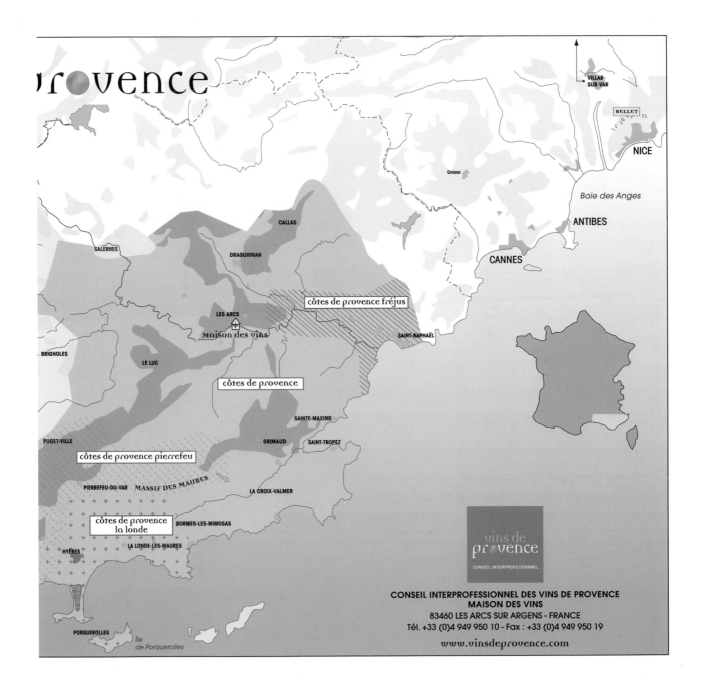

provence

VILLAR-SUR-VAR

BELLET

NICE

Baie des Anges

ANTIBES

Grasse

CANNES

CALLAS

SALERNES

DRAGUIGNAN

côtes de provence fréjus

LES ARCS

Maison des vins

SAINT-RAPHAËL

BRIGNOLES

LE LUC

côtes de provence

SAINTE-MAXIME

PUGET-VILLE

GRIMAUD

SAINT-TROPEZ

côtes de provence pierrefeu

PIERREFEU-DU-VAR   MASSIF DES MAURES

LA CROIX-VALMER

côtes de provence
la londe

BORMES-LES-MIMOSAS

HYÈRES

LA LONDE-LES-MAURES

vins de
provence
CONSEIL INTERPROFESSIONNEL

PORQUEROLLES

Île
de Porquerolles

CONSEIL INTERPROFESSIONNEL DES VINS DE PROVENCE
MAISON DES VINS
83460 LES ARCS SUR ARGENS - FRANCE
Tél. +33 (0)4 949 950 10 - Fax : +33 (0)4 949 950 19

www.vinsdeprovence.com

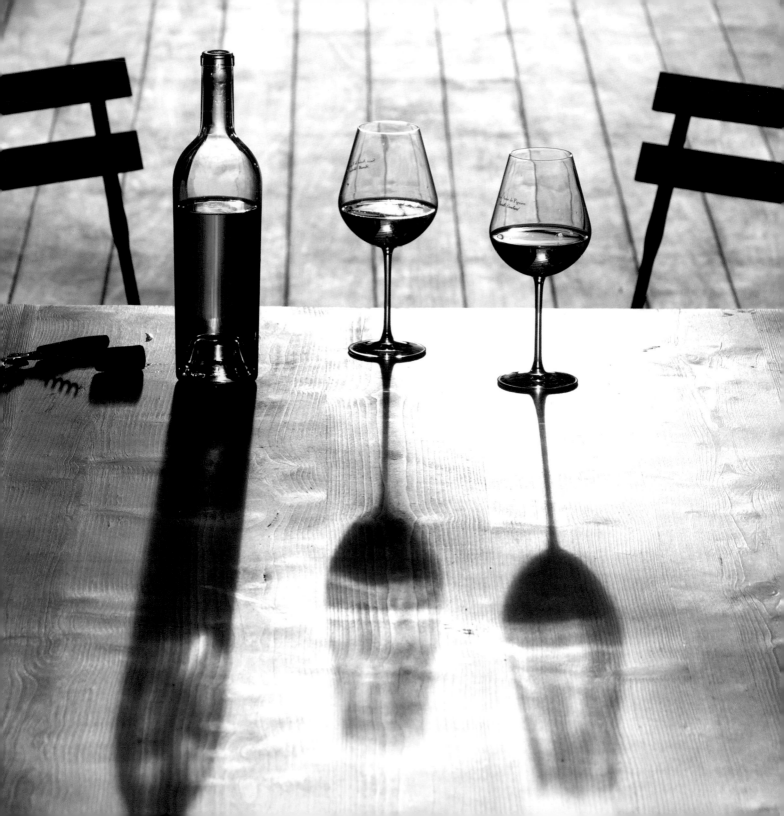

Acknowledgments

We would like to thank the regional and local offices of tourism and the organizations of wine and wine tourism (listed in the Resources section), who provided information and support for this book. In particular, we would like to thank the following individuals for their help and support: Jean Jacques Breban, James de Roany, Valerie Lelong, Jennifer Penna, Cedric Skrzypczak, and Cécile Garcia (Vins de Provence council), Bruno James (regional tourism office of Provence), Isabelle Bremond (Department Office of Tourism Bouches du Rhône); Anne Martel Reison and Julie Peterson (EOC), Marie José Birot and Sophie Bramoullé (Office of Tourism Aix-en-Provence), Franck Sylvestre (Atelier des Chefs), Patricia Montesinos and Laure Pierrisnard (L'Occitane), Anne Garabedian (Gourméditerannée), la Bonne Mère (Marseille), Claude Maniscalco (Office of Tourism Saint-Tropez), Evelyne Bruza-Priebe (Regional Tourism Office Cote d'Azur), Denis Zanon and Caterina Prochilo (Office of Tourism Nice), Gio Sergi (AOC Bellet), Franck Dominique Ranieri (Office of Tourism Grasse), Patricia Mertzig (Office of Tourism Menton), and Elodie Hoarau (Fragonard).

We would also like to thank the chefs who contributed recipes and photos: Jacques Chibois, Xavier Mathieu, Mathias Gervais, Lionel Levy, Christian and Thomas Millo, and Thierry Thiercelin.

Our sincerest gratitude goes to our families and friends for their patience and support.

Index

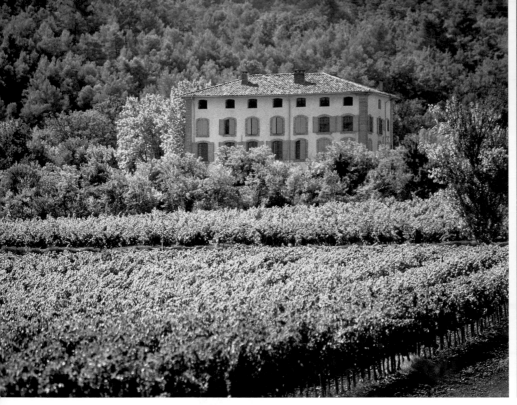
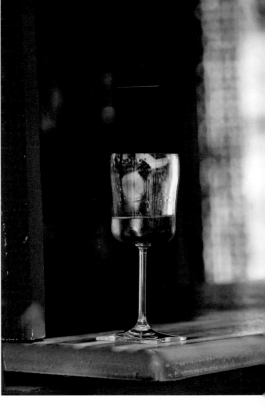

About the Authors

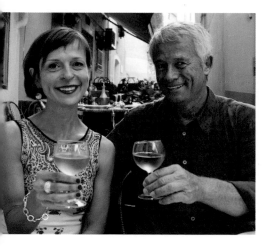

VIKTORIJA TODOROVSKA is a cookbook author and food and wine educator in Chicago. Passionate about the cooking and wines of the Mediterranean, Viktorija explores its culinary treasures through travel and interesting encounters with local cooks, chefs, and wine makers. Enchanted by the culture, foods, and wines of sunny Provence, Viktorija partnered with François Millo to bring to English-speaking readers the richness and beauty of the region.

Viktorija's previous cookbooks, *The Puglian Cookbook: Bringing the Flavors of Puglia Home* (April 2011) and *The Sardinian Cookbook: The Cooking and Culture of a Mediterranean Island* (October 2013), published by Surrey Books, paint vivid pictures of the regions and their culinary traditions. For more information on Viktorija, visit her websites: www.olivacooking.com and www.mywinesmarts.com.

FRANÇOIS MILLO is a photographer and author of several wine books and culinary guides. Born and raised in Provence, François loves his native region, but also the world. After studying agricultural engineering and marketing, he worked internationally for several years including African countries and Mexico. He went on to direct the Regional Union of Bordeaux wines for eight years.

François is fascinated by all cultures and traditions, but his passion for his native region keeps him deeply rooted in the *terroir* of Provence. In 1990, he became director of the Interprofessional Council of Provence Wines, following the rapid development of this viticultural region.

François' recent previous books include *Os rosé e suas harmonizacaoes* (Bocato Brazil 2011), *Les instants du rosé* (Hachette 2010), and *La Provence et ses vins* (FERET, Bordeaux 2005). He is also the coauthor of a comprehensive technical manual on rosé wine, *Le Rosé* (FERET, 2009).